the
Dream Sleeper

A Three-Part Plan for
Getting Your Baby to Love Sleep

CONNER HERMAN AND KIRA RYAN
and the Expert Advisors of Dream Team Baby

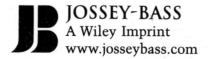

JOSSEY-BASS
A Wiley Imprint
www.josseybass.com

Published by Jossey-Bass
A Wiley Imprint
One Montgomery Street, Suite 1200, San Francisco, CA 94104-4594—www.josseybass.com

Jossey-Bass books and products are available through most bookstores. To contact Jossey-Bass directly call our Customer Care Department within the U.S. at 800-956-7739, outside the U.S. at 317-572-3986, or fax 317-572-4002.

Wiley also publishes its books in a variety of electronic formats and by print-on-demand. Some material included with standard print versions of this book may not be included in e-books or in print-on-demand. If the version of this book that you purchased references media such as CD or DVD that was not included in your purchase, you may download this material at http://booksupport.wiley.com. For more information about Wiley products, visit www.wiley.com.

Library of Congress Cataloging-in-Publication Data
Herman, Conner, date.
   The dream sleeper : a three-part plan for getting your baby to love sleep / Conner Herman and Kira Ryan and the expert advisors of Dream Team Baby.
      p. cm.
   Includes bibliographical references and index.
      ISBN 978-1-118-01842-2 (pbk.); ISBN 978-1-118-18144-7 (ebk); ISBN 978-1-118-18145-4 (ebk); ISBN 978-1-118-18146-1 (ebk)
   1. Infants–Sleep.   2. Parent and infant.   3. Infants–Development.   I. Ryan, Kira, date.
II. Dream Team Baby (Firm).   III. Title.
   BF720.S53H47 2012
   649'.122–dc23
2011044982

Printed in the United States of America
FIRST EDITION
PB Printing   10 9 8 7 6 5 4 3 2 1

To John, Emilia, Carter, and Charlotte. I'm so lucky to have each of you in my life. Thank you for all that you give me and teach me every day. Your smiles and hugs were the sustenance that helped us get this book into the world. Without all of you, so much would not be possible—or fun.
I love you with all of my heart.
—Kira Ryan

To my husband, Brad; our children, Wyatt, McCoy, and Everett; my father, Richard Wyatt, who basically moved into our home so we could finish this book; my mother, Marcia Wyatt, who let my father move in with us; and my in-laws, Sally and Steve Herman, who are always there when I need them. You are the most patient and selfless family I could ever ask for. Thank you for your understanding and belief in me. Without your confidence and support, this book, and our business, would not exist. I love all of you.
—Conner Herman

CONTENTS

PART ONE Get Ready!

Great sleep teaching begins with choice, change,
and flexibility, not a quick fix.

PART TWO Get Set!

The six critical steps in guiding your baby toward sleep success.

PART THREE Get Sleep!

*Where the real work of sleep teaching
begins—and continues.*

We were seated at a table in the back of a nondescript Italian restaurant on the Upper West Side of New York City, talking about sleep. The invitation had come through Kira Ryan, an intelligent, gentle, and good-humored mother of one of my patients whom I had come to know over that past year. At the close of her daughter's checkup one afternoon, Kira had asked if I would be interested in helping her and a friend create a sleep consulting business. Perhaps it was the abundance of sleep questions in my practice that day, perhaps it was the nightly 2:00 A.M. waking with my eleven-month-old son (who had previously slept through the night), or perhaps it was Kira's thoughtful excitement that inspired me to accept the offer. Whatever the reason, I found myself eating dinner that night with two women who were very excited about sleep.

Kira's friend and business partner, Conner Herman, is a warm, dynamic woman. She possesses an unexpected combination of southern graciousness and military-like determination. Kira and Conner described to me how they had met on the streets of New York, instantly connected, and shared their individual struggles with their children's sleep. Conner confessed suffering months of guilt and exhaustion while fruitlessly wading though advice books, Web sites, and the well-meaning suggestions of friends. She told me that she had finally enlisted the help of a sleep consultant, and her family was literally totally transformed by sleep—and I believed her. I believed her partly because Conner radiates trustworthiness and partly because I witness families changed by sleep every day in my pediatric practice.

When Kira subsequently found herself struggling with her daughter's sleep, Conner (in the way only an empathetic best friend can) guided her through the process of helping her daughter learn to sleep. Kira's daughter began sleeping, and her family was transformed as well. Over the next several months, Conner and Kira started helping their friends solve relatively simple sleep issues with great success. They noted both the commonness of sleep problems as well as the unique way they played out in each family. They observed that when given specific knowledge and great empathy, most families had the ability to solve their child's sleep issues, and as they helped more and more families, they came to appreciate the large number of families who struggled with their children's sleep yet didn't know where to go for support and help. It was these observations that led them to the idea of helping families through a business of sleep consultation. I thought their idea was brilliant. They were in search of expertise to deepen their understanding of sleep, and I was all too happy to lend my medical knowledge and perspective.

When I started my pediatric practice, I knew very little about the sleep issues parents face throughout the life of their child. This was not because I skipped that lecture in medical school, suffered from substandard residency training, or failed to realize the importance of sleep. It was because my focus—as for many others during medical training—had been on more acute medical issues. Of course, I understood that no pediatric checkup was complete without a sleep history, and most visits by sick children required inquiry about how sleep had been affected. But solving the typical infant or toddler sleep problem had been at best a back-burner matter for me—until it was not anymore.

Sleep became and remains a central topic of discussion in caring for my patients and their families. Many parents struggle with getting the right amount of sleep for their children, many parents are sleep deprived, and many parents enter my office seeking advice on how to go about changing this pattern.

In this new age of information, most parents have at least some knowledge of the numerous and significant ill effects of sleep loss or deprivation. They may know that sleep loss has cardiovascular effects such as an increased risk for hypertension or decreases in immune responses. They may be aware of the greater risk for mood disorders such as depression and anxiety associated with sleep loss; the substantial impairment in cognitive abilities such as sustained attention, short-term memory, information processing, and school performance; or the increased risk for motor vehicle accidents that accompanies lack of sleep. They may have read about the growing body of research that suggests a link between obesity and sleep loss: both children and adults who sleep less tend to weigh more. Most parents are not without some measure of subjective and objective evidence that sleep is vitally important for both them and their children.

Why, then, are children and their parents not getting the sleep that they need? The reason is that often enough, we find that helping our children to sleep well is not easy. Most of the time, helping our children to sleep requires tolerating some temporary, though significant, discomfort—ours or theirs—in the pursuit of what we now know is the ideal long-term outcome. As a parent, I struggled with this issue, as I know so many of my patients and their families do too.

So this is where Conner, Kira, and the rest of Dream Team Baby come in. Possessing the compassion of a best friend, comprehensive knowledge gleaned from expert consultants, and proven methods and techniques, Conner and Kira give parents everywhere the strength to help their children sleep well. You will wish only that you had read this book sooner.

Amy DeMattia, M.D.

Our ability to help families would not be possible without the smarts and guidance of our incredible group of advisors. Each woman listed here has played a critical role in teaching us everything we know about sleep. We think the world of them, and they are truly the backbone of everything we share in this book. You will see tips from all of these advisors throughout the book.

PEDIATRICIAN Amy DeMattia is a physician at Westside Pediatrics in New York City. Dr. DeMattia is also an assistant clinical professor at the Mount Sinai Medical Center School of Medicine, where she remains active in medical education. She is a graduate of Princeton University and Cornell University Medical College. She completed her pediatric residency, master's in public health, and fellowship in general academic Pediatrics at Mount Sinai Hospital in New York City. Dr. DeMattia has practiced pediatrics for more than ten years and lives in New York City with her husband and two children.

NEUROLOGIST Pantea Sharifi Hannauer is a long-time attending clinical physician at UCLA Medical Center in Los Angeles, where she is recognized as one of the premiere experts in the field of pediatric behavioral and developmental disabilities. Her practice, Pediatric Minds, is scientifically based and

Alexandra K. Photography at PlaydateLosAngeles.com.

promotes behavioral treatment or other preventative measures before pursuing medical or pharmaceutical interventions. The mother of two children, Pantea understands the challenges associated with parenting today.

PSYCHOLOGIST   Ingrid Schweiger is a New York City–based licensed psychotherapist. For the past thirty years, she has specialized in helping adults and couples deal with depression, anxiety, relationship concerns, parenting problems, and addictions. Her unique programs for families have been recognized by the American Association for Marriage and Family Therapy. She received her doctorate in counseling psychology at the University of Massachusetts. She is the author of *Self-Esteem for a Lifetime: Raising a Successful Child from the Inside Out.*

LACTATION CONSULTANT   Carolyn Migliore is a registered nurse with a master's degree in maternal child health nursing with more than thirty years of experience. She is a part-time lactation consultant at New York–Presbyterian Hospital, where she works with new mothers and babies during their hospital stay. She also has a large private practice as a certified Lamaze instructor and lactation consultant and infant massage instructor for clients in the New York City area.

BEHAVIOR ANALYST   Britt Moore is a Board Certified Behavior Analyst with extensive experience in treating children with autism spectrum disorders, focusing on parent training. Since 2001, she has been working with children with developmental delays and their families, using specific approaches to encourage appropriate behaviors in their home and surrounding communities. This approach teaches parents how to encourage appropriate behaviors in their home environment. She received her master's degree in applied behavior analysis from Western Michigan University and resides with her family in St. Paul, Minnesota.

NURSE PRACTITIONER   Meg Zweiback is a pediatric nurse practitioner with more than thirty years of specialized experience in behavioral and developmental pediatrics. She operates a private consulting practice in the San Francisco Bay Area and is an associate clinical professor of family health care nursing at the University of California, San Francisco. Among the parenting books she has written are *Keys to Parenting Your One-Year-Old*, *Keys to Preparing and Caring for Your Second Child*, and *Keys to Toilet Training*. Her practical advice to parents can be found at www.bringingupkids.com.

Welcome! We're so happy to help you teach your baby how to love sleep. We know you can do it!

This book has three parts. Parts One and Two are directed to all sleep-deprived parents. The chapters in Part One provide an introduction to sleep and an overview of how your baby's sleep changes over the first two years of his or her life. Part Two then teaches the six critical steps to sleep success. Even families that are not ready to sleep-teach can use these steps to get better sleep for their family now. And if you absolutely cannot, under any circumstances, stand to hear your baby cry, we recommend you use only Parts One and Two of this book.

Part Three is for families that are ready to sleep-teach. You will learn our Dream Team Baby approach to help your baby get eleven to twelve hours of sleep at night, instructions on the specific methods we use with our clients, and what to do when you hit the inevitable bumps. Even if you feel 100 percent ready to start sleep teaching today, please do not jump directly to Part Three. Our whole method is based on the principle that fixing sleep is not just about the act of falling sleep. If you skip Parts One and Two, you might miss an important step that could interfere with your success in implementing the plan in Part Three.

This book also has several real-life sleep stories about different families who struggled with sleep (some who may just sound a lot like you). As mothers, we know that hearing from people in your exact situation can be incredibly motivating. Fortunately, some of the families we've worked with have offered to contribute their stories and share bits of advice that kept them focused on fixing their baby's sleep. You'll see their words sprinkled throughout the book, and we hope it feels comforting to have fellow parents cheer you on as you help your child learn to love sleep as much as their children do now.

Throughout this book, we try to be as sensitive to nontraditional families as possible; however, in a few instances, we suggest that "Dad" put the baby to bed or "Mom" might be feeling a certain way. Please understand that we are referring to specifically separate roles in these cases and not suggesting that sleep teaching works only in traditional families.

If you're struggling with sleep issues with your children, we hope you read this entire book and use our advice to help your family. But no matter what method you end up using, know in your heart that you're a great parent because you care enough to try to make things better for your family.

ACKNOWLEDGMENTS

This book would not be possible without a virtual stadium full of amazing people: fellow parents, coworkers, friends, family, and, of course, children.

We first extend our heartfelt gratitude to our clients. It was, and is, a privilege to work with you. We're incredibly honored you trust us with the most important treasure in your lives, your children.

To our amazing team of advisors—Amy, Pantea, Ingrid, Carolyn, Britt, and Meg (learn more about them in the Meet Our Dream Team section)—you not only helped us create our approach, you helped us grow as parents. You keep us thinking and on our toes when it comes to the latest thinking in pediatric care. None of this would be possible without all of you, and those big brains and hearts of yours.

To our dedicated, tireless team of consultants over the years—Natalie, Traci, Paula, Elizabeth, Tania, Nina, Jennifer, and Tara—you transform lives. Thank you for your hard work and shared enthusiasm for sleep. We consider each of you an angel and know your clients would agree.

To Katina, who is much, much more than a content specialist, thank you for pulling long hours and for your excellent ideas along the way. Your perspective and your own parenting issues helped us create something we hope will connect with many people.

To our editor, Kate; our agent, Frank; and the teams at Jossey-Bass and the Literary Group, we are so thankful you saw promise in our idea. Your partnerships were the easiest of marriages: mutually respectful, efficient, and fun. Maybe we'll even do this again someday.

To our friends, whose support and encouragement was very much appreciated and treasured. Thank you, thank you, thank you. We are sorry for the birthdays we missed while trying to meet our deadline and promise to make it up to you in the years to come.

And finally, to our amazing extended families who served as pinch sitters, provided meal delivery services, and also served as our own grassroots PR professionals. Thank you for your time and love before this process, during this process, and forevermore.

Sweet dreams,
Conner and Kira

the
Dream Sleeper

A Perfect Little World— Until Sleep Deprivation Knocks at Your Door

Your baby is finally here! Put aside the stretch mark belly cream, pack up those worn-out maternity pants, and relish how easy it is to get up from the couch. Your baby is healthy and cute as a button—and you're getting the hang of multitasking like you never knew possible. All is right within your own little universe.

But before you know it, the first few months with your sweet baby have passed, and sleep deprivation is setting in. You've tried a few sleep tricks from moms you've met, but your baby still won't sleep through the night. So you let your baby nap in your arms, or with you, even on you, but you wonder if you're creating a bad sleeper for life. Enter guilt and self-doubt: *Why can't I figure this out? Is there something wrong with my baby? What am I missing here?*

You turn to the Internet, ask more friends, and buy books that you hope have the answer. But now you're more confused than ever before. There seems to be so much conflicting advice. Somewhere in the back of your head, you hear those ominous words from countless other parents: "You will never sleep well again." And you start to believe it's true.

We've been where you are. In our own personal quests for sleep shortly after the births of our first children, we read and attempted just about every method out there. It was a long, lonely, and weary road, but fortunately, we both found sleep for our families. Our collective experiences with poorly sleeping children inspired us to help other parents like us—parents like you.

At first we didn't know how to fix sleep, so we enlisted the help of brilliant doctors, therapists, and other experts in the medical and mental health communities. Sleep is affected by a lot of different things, and we wanted everyone to bring their best thinking to the table. Together we defined some new ways of thinking about sleep principles and came up with a framework that could be simple and adaptable for parents, regardless of their parenting styles, child's preferences, or even age of the children.

Like a lot of other sleep professionals, we treat sleep in the same way that nutritionists approach food. The key to maintaining healthy sleeping and dietary results is proper education and consistency through the challenging times. Of course, ice cream is great—but it isn't great in large quantities, day in and day out. Rocking a baby to sleep in your arms feels great, but if you have to do it for every sleep cycle seven times every night, no one is going to be happy—particularly the baby.

In this book, we put sleep in terms you can understand and relate to. More important, we also help you do everything in your power to make teaching your baby how to sleep as easy as possible for you, your child, and the rest of your family. We invest a lot of time in preparing parents for change and laying important groundwork. For instance, although it may seem as if a child's only sleep problem concerns taking naps, we take a 360-degree view of the child's life. This is how we're able to help so many parents create great sleepers for a lifetime.

You may be reading this to get ready for a baby on the way, or maybe you aren't even certain you're ready to work on fixing sleep right now. Or perhaps you were ready to sleep-teach yesterday. In all of these cases, this book will be very helpful to you.

Our clients encouraged us to write this book because they thought other sleep books they had consulted are either too rigid (limiting parents' intuition) or offer too many confusing or even contradictory choices. The parents we work with want a clear action plan that also considers the needs of their specific situation, and that's what we provide. We hope this book strikes a similar balance of specificity of instruction and flexibility for you and your family.

> The most important thing you can do for your baby is to be a happy, healthy parent. When you stop being happy, it's a signal that something needs to change.

As you read this book, you'll learn how to

+ Foster good general sleep habits (like establishing a routine and sticking to a schedule) until the time you're ready to sleep-teach in deeper detail
+ Prepare your baby environmentally, physically, and emotionally for learning to sleep
+ Understand, accept, and grow in your role as a parent throughout the teaching process
+ Identify when sleep teaching is working and when it's not
+ Interact with your baby at night when she needs you and help your baby understand when she doesn't need you
+ Create a great sleeper for life (while incorporating some flexibility into your life too)

We're honored to be your partners on this journey of discovery—one that will change how you see yourself as a parent while having a positive impact on your baby's perception of the world.

What could be better?

PART ONE

Get Ready!

Great sleep teaching begins with choice, change, and flexibility, not a quick fix.

CHAPTER 1

What You Should Know Before You Start

So, how do we get started in teaching our baby to sleep through the night?" That's the question most new parents want answered immediately. We're action-oriented people ourselves so we understand their desire to get to the point. However, if we just told you what to do in this first chapter, you wouldn't understand the motivation and science behind what you are doing to teach your baby to sleep—which means it probably wouldn't work, especially in the long term. It may feel impossible, but we encourage you to take your time because our goal is to help you get your child to love sleep for the rest of her life.

Keys to Zzzs

- **Sleep teaching is probably easier than you think.**
  But it can also be complicated in ways you likely haven't yet considered.

- **Before you choose a sleep teaching method, decide whether you're ready to begin.** Are you emotionally ready to deal with some crying and physically ready with a separate space for sleep-teaching your baby?

- **Every method has pros and cons.** The key is to find what works best for you and your family.
- **Practice consistency.** It's the most important ingredient when working on sleep.
- **Ride the challenges.** Sleep teaching can be difficult, but it offers a lifetime of benefits.

Facts About Sleep

Teaching your baby to sleep isn't rocket science. If it were, we wouldn't be in this business. By the time you get to the end of this book, you'll be amazed at how truly easy it is to teach your baby how to be a great sleeper. But to keep your baby sleeping well, it's important to understand all the whys, so we'll need to lay the groundwork before you start sleep teaching. (*Spoiler alert:* We're eventually going to tell you to let your baby fall asleep by herself in her crib.)

Sleep Fact #1: **After four months of age, the optimal amount of sleep for your baby is eleven to twelve hours each night—and it's entirely achievable.**

When we tell exhausted parents we can help their children sleep eleven to twelve hours each night, they usually respond as if we just told them they won a lottery. It's a mixture of shock, disbelief, and wonder. Yet this amount of sleep is entirely possible, even for babies who have been challenging sleepers from the start.

Four months of age is a great time to start working toward this ideal amount of sleep. It's true that some children are capable of learning sooner, but it's hard to know if you have one of those babies, and if you don't, you are going to find yourself running uphill the entire time. The first few months with a new baby require a lot of work. Make it easier on yourself by waiting until the four-month mark. Make sure this is your child's gestationally corrected age (see the box). The sailing will be a lot smoother for everyone.

Figuring Out Your Baby's Gestational Age

Paying attention to your baby's age when you apply our advice is very important, especially if your baby was born before your due date. To figure out your baby's gestational age, subtract her birth date from your due date. Then subtract that time from your baby's actual age. The resulting age is your baby's gestational age. So if your baby is four months old but was born three weeks early, her gestational age is three months, one week.

Sleep Fact #2: Independent sleep is a learned skill for most. Teaching takes preparation.

One thing all of our advisors agreed on was that independent sleep is a learned skill for many babies—and setting the stage for proper learning takes proper planning.

Teaching a young child to sleep is not something parents should start at 3:00 A.M. It's tempting to do it then because it's about this point in the night when many parents desperately want a change and are highly motivated to start this work. However, it's also when parents can barely see through their exhausted haze, much less think clearly. Some of the most important aspects of sleep teaching must be addressed before parents put their child in the crib to learn to sleep for the first time. If this important preparation is omitted, parents may be asking their child to overcome obstacles that have nothing to do with sleep.

Here's an analogy. If you're thinking about running a marathon, you would never just finish up dinner on a random Tuesday night and declare, "Okay, it's on! I'm hitting this marathon right now." If you simply started running, chances are you'd stop pretty soon in because you'd realize you weren't quite ready for a variety of reasons. Your feet hurt because you didn't put your running shoes on. You're tired after a day at work. Your stomach is turning circles because you just ate a huge meal. You actually have no idea when you're supposed to stop because you haven't mapped out a path. We can come up many more reasons that you aren't set up for success if you attempt a marathon in this manner. Physiologically you may actually be capable of running a marathon, but your chances of struggling through it and possibly failing increase substantially if you do it on the spur of the moment.

A more reasonable approach would be to follow a more deliberate path, one more in sync with your body's needs. The run would start in the morning when the sun isn't beating down. You'd carbo-load the night before, wear the proper running attire, and taper off your workouts so you'd have more energy on race day. You might even ask someone special to be at the nineteenth mile, because you know that's when you're going to need a morale boost.

Sleep teaching is the same way. It is best accomplished with planning and proper preparation.

Sleep Fact #3: **Babies believe what we teach them to believe.**

Even from a very young age, our children are able to read us like an open book. They can sense if we're tired or sad. They watch our facial expressions intensely, study our posture, and pay careful attention to the nuances, positive and negative, in our voices. These everyday signals communicate a great deal to our babies.

The same goes for the way we react to the everyday things they do. For example, if you breast-feed your baby every time he wakes up, the baby believes that if he wakes up, he must be fed before he can go back to sleep. No matter how tired he is, this baby is going to wait until his mom comes in to feed him. This baby isn't crying in the middle of the night because he hates waking up alone in his crib; rather, he has been taught to expect his mom to come in when he awakens. This is why it's so important to unite our nonverbal behavior with our actions.

Can you imagine how much anxiety you might feel if every time you opened your eyes throughout the night and looked at the alarm clock, you had to wait for someone to come in and "let" you go back to sleep? You'd absolutely dread waking up. That's how babies feel when they want to sleep but don't know it's within their power to do so. Some parents swear their baby hates to sleep, but we know that's highly unlikely. Once babies are released from their unnecessary dependence on sleep crutches, they generally love to sleep. They become empowered, confident, relaxed, and happy.

Sleep Fact #4: **Crying is a form of communication for your baby.**

It's hard to listen to your baby cry. However, beware of equating your baby's feelings to a situation that would cause you to cry with a similar intensity. To do so is to undermine all the hard work you've done to become an emotionally balanced and reasonable adult (let's all have a moment of silence here for our teenage years).

Here's an experiment. Take a toy away from your baby. In less than a second, this child is going to sound as if his entire world is crumbling before his very eyes. Give the toy back, and as fast as the baby started crying, he stops. Crying for a baby is not the same as it is for us. We know how to reason and use language to voice our feelings. Babies don't have that ability yet, so to show displeasure or get your attention, they cry.

You'll hear us say this several times in this book: not all crying is bad or harmful crying. We get questions from concerned parents who heard or read somewhere that crying was damaging to children. Because of this misinformation and parents' concern, we cover the issue of crying in depth throughout this book: how to interpret cries and how to support a child who is crying.

Very few of us can remain totally unaffected when we hear our child cry. We don't enjoy listening to crying, but here's our (and the Dream Team Baby board's) take on it:

+   *Crying can be a way for babies to blow off steam and vent frustrations.* Preventing children from experiencing all of life's frustrations is not healthy or possible.

+   *When babies are tired and dependent on us for sleep, they often cry and fuss for help.* Teaching them how to sleep on their own may involve a few days of frustrated crying. But after that, they will cry less. Instead of rousing at night and having to cry for Mom to wake up, put her robe on, go get him, make a bottle, feed him, change his diaper, rock a little bit, and then he can go back to sleep, your baby stops crying because now all he needs to do is close his eyes and go back to sleep. It's a great deal for us and a better deal for your baby. A few days of controlled crying in the name of sleep teaching will lead to less total crying overall.

+   *Research overwhelmingly demonstrates the extensive and long-term benefits of sleep.* But we don't know of any studies showing that controlled crying conducted in a loving family environment (stable, positive interactions during the day) is harmful to babies or young children.

Sleep Fact #5: **Parental consistency is critical to helping children sleep better.**

Many parents know that consistency is important, but one area many people overlook is internal consistency—truly, consistently believing that your child can succeed. When you are insecure about your baby's readiness to learn to sleep, your ability to stay mentally in the game will be limited.

We know some of you are not ready or willing to allow your baby to be frustrated for any reason right now. That's totally fine, but if that's the case, we strongly urge you not to teach your baby to sleep right now. You can still help with your baby's quality of sleep; read Chapters Two through Eight, and you'll immediately put your family on a track to improved sleep. Also, if you have a time limit to how long you can support a child who may be frustrated (if you are thinking, for example, "Let's try it tonight and see how it goes"), then this is also probably not the time to begin the full approach.

Is Now Really the Right Time?

You're exhausted. You know your baby can be a better sleeper. You're ready to start sleep teaching tonight. We can totally relate to that. But being eager and exhausted doesn't necessarily mean you're ready.

It's important for you to be absolutely sure that now is the right time to sleep-teach. Starting and stopping is hard on parents and even harder on children. Do your entire family a favor by asking yourself the following questions:

+ *Is my baby old enough for sleep teaching?* Many parents make the mistake of starting to sleep-teach before their children are physically or cognitively ready to learn. You'll have the easiest time if you wait until your child is four months old.

- *Are you okay with your current sleep situation?* We talk to parents all the time who say they're okay with their baby sleeping in the crib for the first part of the night and cosleeping safely for the second part of the night. If that's the case, now may not be the right time to change. Wait until you're really ready to change things for good.

- *Can your lives accommodate sleep teaching right now?* Change is hard, and stressful events can affect your focus and stamina when teaching your baby to sleep independently. If you're in transition right now or experiencing a loss of some sort, now may not be the best time to add more stress.

- *Is your partner supportive of sleep teaching?* Sleep teaching can be overwhelming and isn't something you should attempt alone. If your partner is adamantly opposed to sleep teaching, work on getting on the same page first.

You're Ready: Now Which Method Should You Choose?

If you've determined you're ready to help your baby's sleep improve, the next big decision is choosing the right method or approach for your family.

Parts One and Two of this book will give you tips for sleep teaching no matter what approach you use. Part Three takes you through our specific approach to sleep teaching, but there are many methods other than ours. One difference between our approach and the others is our focus on preparing your baby for change and looking at your baby's entire living situation so you can fix any sleep inhibitors before you start working on sleep. We all try to establish some sort of discipline and guidelines for our children during the day, yet many of us struggle to apply the same logic at night. Setting limits, not giving into tantrums, ensuring our children aren't hitting others or grabbing their toys: these are all similar to setting sleep boundaries. Setting sleep boundaries is more difficult, however, because it feels different at night. It's dark, everyone's exhausted, and when you hear your baby rouse after a few hours, it is easy to worry he may be uncomfortable or hungry. But once you have a plan and the right environment in place, fixing sleep isn't as challenging as you may think, mainly because you've set your child up for success.

Setting your baby up for success means that when the day comes to ask your baby to sleep through the night, you're confident your child is ready to learn how to sleep. You and your partner are a team, and you've cleared your schedule for the next two weeks so you can keep everything as consistent as possible. Having a strong foundation and a solid start gives parents confidence and increases their potential to be consistent and positive teachers for their babies.

Focus on the Benefits

If you are worried that sleep teaching will be too hard for you and your family, try focusing on the benefits you'll start to see once you help your child achieve independent sleep:

+ *Increased attention span.* Everyone knows it's hard to concentrate when you're tired. A number of recent studies have reported a relationship between the attention span of school-age children and their sleep schedule. Imagine what it's like to be a baby. Everything from a tongue movement to focusing on an object requires a lot of effort and work. It's not uncommon for us to see improvements in language, feeding coordination, and emotional control once the baby starts sleeping well. And it should feel good to know that you took things into your own hands to help your baby be the best she can possibly be instead of struggling against the odds.

+ *Improved self-esteem.* It may conflict with your natural instincts, but children love to do things for themselves. Your baby spends her life being taken care of, so when she realizes that something is in her control, her joy is absolute.

+ *Happier parents.* A lot of times, exhausted parents are so tired and desperate for the day to end that they end up wishing daytime hours away. Sleep deprivation can dull the entire parenting experience, including intimacy and your relationship with your partner. It's hard to enjoy each moment when you're counting down to naptime or bedtime.

Sweet Dreams!

There are many reasons that solving your child's sleep problems is good for your family. In fact, the only reason we can think of for not starting sleep teaching right away is that it's not the right time for your family. If you know you can't be consistent or see it through right now, it's better to wait.

Now let's take a closer look at what sleep really means to your baby.

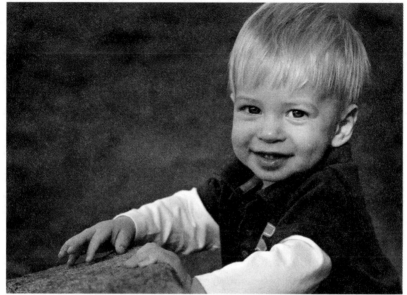

Angela Bruno Photography.

Fixing Sleep Gave Me Confidence and Fulfillment

ROBIN M., MOM TO OWEN

Owen arrived after long struggles to get pregnant. There was a miscarriage, several failed in vitro fertilizations, and then finally, miracle of miracles, I became pregnant. I was never one of those women who always knew she wanted to have a baby one day. In fact, I didn't really want a child until I married my husband. So I was perfectly content before and then just over the moon when I became pregnant. It was as if I had been given everything I could ever want.

I didn't have a lot of experience with kids, and I had never even changed a diaper until my baby arrived. To say I was overwhelmed when the baby finally arrived would be an understatement!

17

Owen was born by C-section, and he was of course the most beautiful thing I had ever seen. But I struggled after his birth with postpartum depression on a pretty serious level. I had to take anti-depressants. I often wish I could have Owen all over again because truthfully, I almost don't remember a lot from his early life. I also became pretty ill with stomach and back issues, so I was a mess! There was no true instinct that ever kicked in, and I was overwhelmed.

Since Owen wanted to nurse every three hours, I was getting only spotty sleep at night; in the daytime, he would nap only in my arms. I couldn't get much rest and was getting frustrated, so I read every book on the topic, and the only consistent message I got was that sleep was vital for the baby. I knew that the situation needed to change, that it could be better for him, but the books were so full of contradictory information. I just needed someone to tell me what to do—and mostly, that it was going to be okay. The experts on Dream Team did that for me.

We got through the rough patch relatively quickly, and it was almost as though Owen went to sleep and I finally woke up. He's a happy little guy, and you can see a glimmer in his eyes. And I started feeling more confident as a mom. I was finally able to say, "Yes, my baby sleeps through the night!" It really changed my world—and he's now a great sleeper. Having a schedule for the day really helps, and it was exactly what I needed.

Without sleep, there's very little enjoyment in life, and everything looks so bleak. Fixing sleep gave me my life back, and saved us all from a potentially dreadful situation. As new moms, we can have such low expectations that a baby not sleeping becomes a truth—and that's actually so far from the truth.

Sleep Science 101

Understanding a few essential sleep principles before you make any changes to your life will help you be a much better teacher for your child. Understanding how sleep develops and works will give you the confidence to remain calm. And as a bonus, you may even learn a few terms in this chapter you can use to dazzle others (like your in-laws!). Now who's the smartest parent in the room? It's you, of course!

Keys to Zzzs

- There are two main stages of sleep: non-REM, or "quiet," sleep and REM, or "active," sleep. These sleep stages are not easily differentiated until approximately eight weeks of age.
- Day and night mean nothing to babies until they start to produce melatonin, around the six- to eight-week mark. Until then, sleep is likely equally divided between day and night.
- Sleep changes over time. Around eight to twelve weeks, children start to sleep longer stretches, and some begin sleeping

through the night on their own. Four months of age is when you can be confident that your baby can sleep eleven to twelve hours a night, plus daytime naps.

- **Children wake up at night, usually multiple times.** This is a problem only when children who are old enough to get back to sleep on their own can't do so without their parents' help. This is often referred to as having a negative sleep association.

- **Some children have medical issues that affect sleep.** We'll discuss these conditions so you can be aware of them before beginning to sleep-teach.

- **Safety is always most important.** We cover unsafe sleeping practices so that you can make wise choices without compromising your baby's well being.

~~~~~~

What Happens While Babies Sleep

Picture your baby sleeping. She looks so peaceful and beautiful, but what's really happening as she sleeps? Although it may seem a little clinical to delve into the physiology of what's occurring while your baby's asleep, you need to understand a few sleep basics. This information will also help you understand why we recommend holding off on sleep teaching until your baby is at least four months old—and at the same time help you not feel guilty for any "poor" sleep habits you seem to be encouraging until this time.

When we sleep, we transition, or cycle, through two different modes of sleep: quiet sleep (non–rapid eye movement, or non-REM, sleep) and active sleep (REM sleep). In the period of quiet sleep, the body slows down all of its metabolic functioning (heart rate, breathing rate) and restores itself. Quiet sleep has four stages, which range from drowsy and light-stage sleep (stages 1 and 2) to deeper-stage sleep (stages 3 and 4). During REM sleep, we dream.

Multiple studies have shown that adequate sleep and regular sleep-and-wake patterns are associated with better overall development in children because each stage has a specific purpose (Spruyt and others, 2008). When babies get the sleep they need, their bodies and minds can do what they're supposed to do. For example, during REM sleep, your baby's brain is basically practicing to be awake. Think about it as a dress rehearsal for daytime brain functioning. During REM, babies outwardly appear active or almost restless. Internally the brain is busy making new connections and processing all the sounds, events, and images your baby experienced throughout the day. REM sleep is also when the brain gets its resupply of neurotransmitters, or brain hormones, like serotonin and dopamine that regulate attention span, coordination, and mood.

"Some of the telltale signs a child is in REM sleep include eyelid twitching, body movements, grimacing, sucking, smiling, or sniffling. It may not look restful to you, but remember, it's a good thing. It shows your child's brain is actively developing. The amount of movement your baby does during sleep has nothing to do with how restful or restorative your child's sleep is."

—DR. PANTEA SHARIFI HANNAUER,
CHILD NEUROLOGIST

The stages of deep sleep are equally as crucial for your child's brain development. Deep sleep is the opposite of REM sleep. If your brain during REM is, say, Times Square in New York City on New Year's Eve, then your brain in deep sleep is a city blackout. Everything has shut down: the heart rate drops, digestion and respiration slow, and neurotransmitters go silent. The whole body and brain are on a yoga retreat, and their cell phones are turned off. The more quality deep sleep the brain gets, the more energy the brain and body have to function when awake.

Because getting good sleep has such beneficial impacts on children, we can understand why everything begins to break down when children (and adults, for that matter) do not get adequate amounts of each stage of sleep. Even if your child doesn't seem to be excessively sleepy, insufficient amounts of sleep can still present in a number of ways:

+ Behavioral or learning problems
+ Hyperactivity
+ Restlessness
+ Poor concentration
+ Impulsivity
+ Aggressiveness
+ Irritability
+ Depression or sadness
+ Decreased immunity

Research also shows that poor napping habits can have some negative consequences. Naps may comprise only a small percentage of your baby's total sleep, but naptime sleep cycles have periods of REM and deep sleep too. Therefore, the results of studies pertaining to benefits of healthy daytime sleep are similar to the results of healthy nighttime sleep (Schwichtenberg, Anders, Vollbrecht, and Poehlmann, 2011). Such studies show that daytime sleep is essential to neurological development in babies and young children; it helps them consolidate information and promotes long-term memory (Bootzin et al., 2009).

It's clear that getting good sleep is important and that sleep teaching is not just about the parents being tired and "done" with the nighttime feedings. Instead, sleep teaching is about recognizing the critical role both REM and deep sleep play in your baby's development and helping your baby achieve the maximum amount of rest so he can be the best that he can be. Fortunately, poor sleeping habits are usually a result of a miscommunication between the baby and the parents, which means that you can fix them.

"Getting the appropriate amount of sleep, including REM and deep sleep, will help children with developmental delays or behavioral issues do better. In my practice, we make sure the sleep is under control first, so the child has every advantage possible to get the most out of their therapy sessions."

—DR. PANTEA SHARIFI HANNAUER,

CHILD NEUROLOGIST

How Much Sleep Babies Need

As we see in our work with families, no two children are the same. So while it's true that some children need less sleep than others, it's also hard to know if your child is one who truly needs less sleep or is just better at functioning with less sleep. How can you know for sure?

If your child isn't getting the recommended amount of sleep, we think it's best to assume he needs more. You may be shocked at the transformation that occurs in your child once he does. Most children over four months of age benefit from consistently getting at least eleven to twelve hours of sleep a night. You may not always see the benefits manifested, but good things are happening nevertheless. Keep the sleep targets in Table 2.1 as your goal. And relax. We've helped many children get these ideal amounts of sleep, even when their parents thought it was an impossible feat.

How Sleep Changes in the First Year

A child's sleep patterns and sleeping abilities change tremendously in the first year of life, although what's "normal" at this age can vary. Some babies sleep through the night, while others sleep in shorter bursts around the clock. Even the same baby can have very different nights back-to-back for no apparent reason.

Birth to Two Months Old: Sleeping Here, There, and Everywhere

We are the only species of animal born without a fully formed brain. When we are born, our brains have not yet begun to use their

Table 2.1 Sleep Targets	
Age[a]	Ideal Sleep Amounts
0 to 4 months	15 to 18 hours total (in a 24-hour period)[b]
4 to 6 months	11 to 12 hours nighttime plus 3 to 4 hours daytime (in three naps)
6 to 12 months	11 to 12 hours nighttime plus approximately 2 to 3.5 hours daytime (in two naps)
12 to 18 months	11 to 12 hours nighttime plus approximately 1.5 to 3 hours daytime (in one or two naps)
18 to 36 months	11 to 12 hours nighttime plus approximately 1.5 to 3 hours daytime (in one nap)

[a]If your child was born prematurely, ensure you are using your child's gestationally corrected age. A box in Chapter One explains how to do the calculations.
[b]Most children under three to four months are able to stay awake for only 1.5 to 2.5 hours at a time and sometimes for only 1 hour at a time.

cerebral cortex, where memory and attention reside. Newborns use only their brain stems and therefore are able to do only very basic things like sleep and eat; even their body movements are primarily driven by reflexes. That's the reason it seems as if your child sleeps the first month away. It's essentially all she can do. Her mind needs the sleep to keep growing, so it will be ready to help her body start doing cool tricks when she's physically more mature.

Even the way newborns sleep is underdeveloped. During the first one to two months of life, babies are incapable of deep sleep. They cycle between light sleep and REM sleep until around eight weeks of age, when deeper sleep starts to appear. Most newborns do not have trouble falling asleep. That's the upside. The downside is that because they are always in lighter stages of sleep, they do not generally stay asleep for very long stretches.

Newborns can't tell the difference between night and day because they do not yet have a circadian rhythm. This is the twenty-four-hour biological cycle that tells us daytime is for activity and night is for sleep. This means you'll be up a lot because their sleep is more equally distributed between day and night. Around six weeks, babies begin to produce the hormone melatonin, a natural neurotransmitter that helps establish a normal sleep-wake cycle. Melatonin, produced by the pineal gland in the brain, helps set the body's circadian rhythm.

That's a lot of change in two months. Since all babies develop in slightly different ways and at different rates, we urge you to resist the temptation to compare your baby to others of the same age. There's a wide range of what's normal.

Two to Four Months Old: Sleep Consolidation and Regulation (But Also Possible Regression)

At the two-month mark, something major has happened: your baby's brain stem has started communicating with his cerebral cortex, a process called *myelination*. This developmental milestone allows your baby to start forming memories so he can start to recall past events (for example, "I made this sound, and my mommy picked me up").

By three months of age, more regular sleep rhythms start kicking in. Babies are now capable of all four stages of quiet sleep, including the deepest stages.

At this point, some children begin sleeping longer stretches, while babies who previously were perfectly sound sleepers may all of a sudden become incredibly restless. One of the reasons this occurs is that some children think they should let you know whenever they are awake. They now remember how you responded the last time and will call for you to repeat the action. Although it's true that a baby's sleep ability at three months is a good predictor of the kind of sleeper he is predisposed to being, it doesn't mean that he can't learn to be a sound sleeper. Rather, you might have to be more organized or structured about how you teach your child to sleep and how you keep him on track.

Babies of this age are better able to self-regulate and do some amount of self-soothing because they are now functioning with more of their cerebral cortex instead of only their brain stem. But remember that just because a child doesn't pick up on self-soothing skills on his own doesn't mean he can't be great at it with a little practice and encouragement.

Children start to be on a more predictable schedule at this age. Although they may not be the same day to day, generally most children need to sleep after every one and a half to two hours of being awake.

Four Months Old: Ready for Independence

The four-month mark is a magical moment in time when it comes to sleep:

+ *Your baby's sleep cycles are established.* Babies are able to sleep at predictable and longer stretches at night and take regular naps.
+ *Her brain development is maturing.* Babies can now recall past events so that once they learn something, they can recreate a similar experience; for example, they can remember that sucking on their thumb to calm down for sleep felt good.
+ *He has improved physical control.* This development allows babies to be more purposeful in their movements, and their coordination is getting better each day. More physical control makes self-soothing easier because they have more soothing options at their disposal.
+ *She has gained weight and has greater stomach capacity.* Babies are able to consolidate their feedings: they can eat enough during the day so they don't need to eat at night. Helping a baby get

the right nutrition during the day can involve doing some home-work to help shift nighttime feeds to daytime, but it is entirely possible for healthy children who are four months and older. Typically any prior gastrointestinal and reflux issues will have resolved themselves or been managed by the four-month mark.

Four to Twenty-Four Months Old: The Prime Sleep Teaching Zone

Four to twenty-four months is the ideal time to sleep-teach your child: her brain will be ready to absorb the concepts, and her body will be able to sustain her for longer periods without your help.

There are only a few reasons that a child might not be capable of learning to sleep on his or her own at this point. These are serious conditions that you would likely know about, not just an everyday stuffy nose or virus. Sleep apnea (your baby might stop breathing in the middle of the night), epilepsy, heart conditions requiring equip-ment, and failure-to-thrive situations are serious and could interfere with sleep teaching. Occasionally babies have minor medical issues, like ear infections or a stomach virus, but once your baby is healthy again, she'll be ready to learn.

dream team

"When it comes to helping families with sleep problems, I tell parents: 'Little kids, little problems. Big kids, big problems.' The sooner you help your child, the easier it will be for everyone."

—DR. AMY DEMATTIA, PEDIATRICIAN

Why Fixing Sleep Is Confusing to Us and Our Babies

Pop quiz: You'll know you've created a great sleeper when your baby stops waking up at night. True or false?

Answer: False. Even great sleepers wake up at night.

Nighttime sleep is a rolling combination of lighter sleep, REM sleep, deeper sleep, and wakefulness. When babies are transitioning between cycles or if they are in lighter stages of sleep, they sometimes rouse. And if your baby rouses, it's natural for her to call for you if you've always helped her fall asleep. The reason is that she's tired and wants to go back to sleep, and she believes she needs your help to do this.

A child between four and twelve months old will have approximately eleven to thirteen sleep cycles a night, each about sixty minutes based on eleven to twelve hours of nighttime sleep. Figure 2.1 shows what a typical night might look like for a baby this age. A child between one and three years old will have approximately seven to nine sleep cycles per night that are about ninety minutes each based on eleven to twelve hours of nighttime sleep. Figure 2.2 shows what a typical night might look like for a baby this age.

Figure 2.1 Nighttime Sleep Cycle Example, Ages Four to Twelve Months

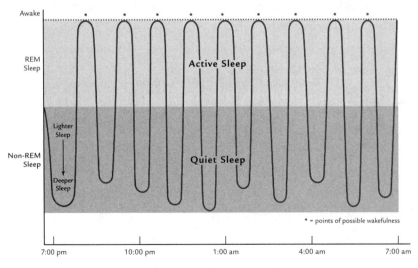

Note: This is a simplification of what happens at night. Actual sleep cycles vary from child to child.

Figure 2.2 Nighttime Sleep Cycle Example, Ages One to Three Years

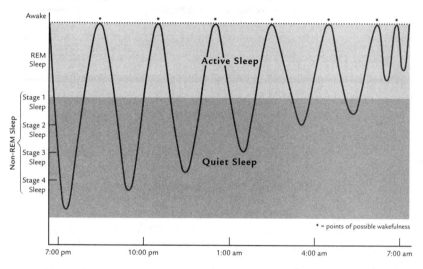

Note: This is a simplification of what happens at night. Actual sleep cycles will vary from child to child.

To make things clear about what happens for your child at night, let's first consider your own sleep. What do you do when you wake up in the middle of the night? You probably open your eyes and notice it's still dark. So you turn your head and see that the clock says 3:15 A.M. If you're like us, you do a very quiet victory celebration that there's still some time to catch some more Zzzs and roll into your favorite position as you close your eyes and drift off to sleep. Maybe you also rubbed your feet together or arranged your sheets in a particular way. But regardless of what you did, no one taught you how to do it. Somewhere along the way, you discovered what felt good to you and did it on your own.

What we just described is called a *positive sleep association.* A sleep association is a condition that you personally associate with falling asleep. It is positive when an individual can create that situation without any outside help. For most adults, sleep associations are so natural that we don't even think about them.

Babies who aren't sleeping through the night usually have negative sleep associations—a sleep environment that's provided by an outside, uncontrollable source like a parent. The key to sleep teaching is identifying your child's negative sleep associations and replacing them with positive ones. Most likely, you'll need to remove yourself from your baby's falling asleep process at bedtime.

Positive sleep association: The person is in control of the environment he or she needs to fall asleep.
Negative sleep association: The person requires support from an outside source to fall asleep.

If your child needs you in order to fall asleep at bedtime or during the day, you've unfortunately become part of how he falls asleep. So it makes sense that your baby would believe the same would be true in the middle of the night. This would be like you waking in the night and feeling compelled to poke your spouse and let him or her know you've opened your eyes. It's completely unnecessary, but this is what your baby thinks he needs to do. Your job is to show him he doesn't need to do this anymore. Believe us, he'll be relieved once he realizes he doesn't need to work himself up to let you know he wants to go to back to sleep.

In Part Two of this book, we'll give you specific instructions on how to identify your baby's negative sleep associations, help him discover his own positive sleep associations, and enjoy sleep just as you do.

Sleep Disorders and Unavoidable Sleep Disturbers

Most babies don't have sleep disorders, but some have conditions that can make the process of falling or staying asleep difficult. If your child has any of the following conditions, it doesn't mean you can't have a great sleeper. It just means that you should consult with your doctor before you do any sleep teaching to determine if the condition is under control by medication or other therapy:

+ Gastroesophageal reflux disease, a condition in which stomach contents, liquid or solid, leak back from the stomach into the esophagus, causing irritation, heartburn, and other symptoms. If this is properly managed by your physician before you start working on sleep, your baby can learn to sleep independently.
+ Central nervous system disorders and parasomnias such as night terrors.
+ Asthma and allergies.
+ Obstructive sleep apnea, or when a child briefly stops breathing during sleep.
+ Low weight.
+ Infections.

Of course, some things that can have a negative impact on sleep don't relate to a serious medical condition. For example, teething, a big concern among all parents we work with, can throw a wrench into sleeping for a few days. So can separation anxiety and developmental night wakings, that is, those directly associated with your baby's milestones, such as walking or talking. We'll discuss how to remedy or help alleviate these temporary conditions throughout this book.

Sudden Infant Death Syndrome and Sudden, Unexpected Infant Death

Sudden infant death syndrome (SIDS) is the leading cause of death for babies between one month and one year of age in the United States. Approximately twenty-five hundred U.S. infants die of SIDS every year. These deaths are classified as sudden and unexplained, and they happen while children are sleeping. In addition, there are up to two thousand sudden, unexpected infant deaths (SUID) caused by accidental suffocation or accidents during sleep each year. Environmental hazards such as limited access to air around the face are what most studies believe contribute to these tragic and untimely deaths.

The following conditions can increase your baby's susceptibility to SIDS and SUIDs:

+ *Overheating.* Babies dressed too warmly or swaddled in thick blankets can become too warm. Room temperatures over seventy-two degrees Fahrenheit are not recommended.

+ *Belly sleeping.* Infants who can't roll over on their own shouldn't be allowed to sleep on their stomachs. They're not physically advanced enough to be able to move around and can end up rebreathing their own exhaled air rather than fresh air.

+ *Unsafe bedding.* Blankets and pillows can potentially suffocate children. Babies who sleep in the same bed as their parents also are more likely to die of SIDS because many parents are unwilling to sleep without pillows and sheets.

+ *Second-hand smoke.* Cigarette smoke robs sleeping babies of needed oxygen. It is particularly dangerous for young children.

+ *Uneducated caregivers.* This is often the main culprit of SIDS and SUID-related deaths. Make sure that anyone who cares for your child is aware of the dangers of unsafe sleeping conditions. Everyone responsible for your child (even when you are home) should know prevention guidelines.

When it comes to SUIDs, a recent study found that sleep-deprived adults are more likely to bet on good outcomes and downplay the chances of negative outcomes (Chee et al., 2011). Caffeine may help your attention during the day, but it doesn't fix your increased likelihood toward risk-seeking behaviors when you're tired. If you find yourself taking sleep risks you once told yourself you'd never do (for example, taking a nap with your baby on your overstuffed couch), find a way to get some extra sleep so you can have some perspective and clarity.

Try to give your baby a few minutes of supervised tummy time everyday. This helps builds neck muscles and core strength, which is thought to help reduce the risk of SIDS.

Many organizations are working to understand and prevent SIDS. We highly suggest you visit informative sites like www.sids .org and www.cribsforkids.org to learn more.

"You should always put your child to sleep on her back. However, if she rolls onto her stomach while in her crib, it's safe for her to remain on her stomach. It can be surprising and scary to parents at first, but if babies have the strength to get onto their stomachs by themselves, we presume they have enough strength to move their heads to the side."

—DR. AMY DEMATTIA, PEDIATRICIAN

Sweet Dreams!

Good sleep is central to everyone's well-being, including your own. REM sleep helps you work through emotions and complicated situations. Deep sleep helps your body and mind feel energized, so you can plan fun adventures during the day and be mentally present with your child. If you're a first-time parent, we'll bet you'll reach a new level of satisfaction and happiness with your new role once you catch up on your sleep too.

"Babies are masters of reading your nonverbals, even from a very young age. So if you are constantly exhausted and have to pretend to have fun, your baby is likely on to you."

—MEG ZWEIBACK, PARENTING COACH

PART TWO

Get Set!

The six critical steps in guiding your baby toward sleep success.

CHAPTER 3

Setting the Stage

Even if you can't bear to hear your baby cry, you'll do her a huge service by following the instructions and tips in this chapter. It'll lay important groundwork for creating a great sleeper and most likely improve your child's current sleep situation. It may not be enough to teach your child to sleep eleven to twelve hours a night, but you should see some improvements if your baby is more than four months of age.

Keys to Zzzs

- **Clear the clutter.** Too many things in your baby's crib can distract him.
- **Darken the room.** Sunlight, even in small amounts, can keep your baby awake atnaptime.
- **Add white noise.** It drowns out distracting household noises that can interfere with sleep.
- **Introduce a lovey.** It's more than just a security blanket.
- **Monitor the temperature.** Some rooms can be too hot or too cold; you want one that's just right.

- **Make good crib choices.** Carefully consider safety issues with crib bumpers and double-check crib height.
- **Carve out a separate sleeping space.** This is especially important if your child is sharing a room.

———————————————————————————————

If you're prepared to follow our plan in Part Two, think of this chapter as the mandatory (and incredibly helpful) study session before your child's first major exam. Of course, this isn't a test, but the important tips and instructions in this chapter are the magic that will ensure your family success in teaching your child how to love sleep.

If you do some preparation, perhaps moving a crib and buying some equipment, and possibly push off sleep teaching for a few days while you get ready, you'll ensure you've gone the extra mile to make learning to sleep as easy as possible for your child.

One more thing before we get started: you can start doing this homework for children of any age (minus the lovey) and for almost any method you use, even some cosleeping lifestyles. Our prework is universally helpful.

Revamping Your Child's Sleeping Environment

Many first-time parents fantasize about creating the perfect nursery for their child. We create a magical babyland with miniature-sized monogrammed pillows, sweet stuffed animals, and adorable organic crib linens. We fill the crib with interesting toys, so when our baby rouses in the middle of the night, he might decide to entertain himself. And we think if we make this room so lovely and yummy, our baby will relax and enjoy bedtime. In fact, he might not even realize he's alone at night. Right?

Unfortunately, this process of creating a perfect baby space in our home is more for us than our baby. It's a loving ritual we do to symbolize the space we're about to make in our hearts and lives for our new child. The more effort we put into making our baby's nursery, the more comfortable we feel about this new chapter in our lives.

But the truth is that a perfect-looking nursery doesn't matter to children when they're young. To really make a big difference in your child's sleeping space, we suggest you think about your nursery as a classroom versus a showroom.

Independent sleep is a learned skill for many children, and their bedroom or nursery is where these lessons will be taking place. Your strategy is to set up this space to make learning as easy as possible.

Clear the Clutter

When children are very young, they rely heavily on visual cues to know what you expect from them. So if you put your baby down to sleep in a crib full of soft toys and stuffed animals, she'll understandably believe it's playtime, not sleep time. Also, young children are quite easily stimulated. A mobile that spins and blinks lights in sync with classical music may look pretty tame to you, but to an infant, it's like having her own private laser light show right there in her crib. The same goes for crib aquariums that play music and glow while plastic fish swim around. Try sleeping next to a flat-screen TV that plays music videos all night long, and you'll understand that it's not so restful.

In addition, babies move while they sleep, so there's a chance your baby might accidentally roll into or onto an electronic crib toy and turn it on. That's the baby equivalent of when you forget to turn off your phone and a text message indicator goes off in the middle of the night. You'd turn such distractions off at night, so it makes sense to apply the same courtesy to your baby.

At the end of the day, children don't need artificial entertainment to keep them busy in a crib. They're naturally curious and will find something to do if they're not exhausted; they might grab their toes or look at their fingers, for example. Your child's crib should be clear of everything except for one age-appropriate sleep lovey.

Here's what we recommend you remove from your baby's crib:

+ Crib aquariums
+ Crib mirrors
+ Mobiles
+ Plush toys that crinkle, light up, play music, or vibrate
+ Stuffed animals
+ Pillows and blankets

The idea is to make your baby's crib comfortable, safe, and boring. When your son doesn't see toys, he'll know it's time to sleep, not time to play. Your goal is to make the crib look like a spa, not the local playground.

> You don't have to throw out all those cute crib toys you may have just received at a baby shower. Instead, distribute them in other areas of your home where you do want to communicate the concept of play. Hang the mobile above the changing table, or attach it to a chair. Spruce up a baby gate with a crib aquarium or place the aquarium next to a changing table. These are great toys; they just don't belong in the crib.

Darken the Room

Sunlight is a stimulant. That's why fancy hotel rooms always have thick shades and curtains—so you get better rest. It's easy to wake up to a dark room, assume it's the middle of the night, and see that it's actually 10:00 A.M.

Having a dark room helps us all sleep better. If your child is struggling with naps, a dark room will help her fall asleep faster and stay asleep longer. You may have been given advice from friends or family members who suggest having your baby nap in a sunny room so she becomes a flexible sleeper. We do not subscribe to that theory. Sunlight in a room simply makes it harder for the body to relax and for anyone to settle down and fall sleep.

Also, you will see that one of our principles for teaching babies to sleep is that we create a consistent environment for sleep. Light in rooms without darkening shades will gradually change throughout the night and during naps, which will make the room feel different to your baby and raise questions in her mind about what she should be doing. When your baby has questions, she becomes frustrated, and when she becomes frustrated, she'll cry more.

If you're struggling with sleep, make the room dark for both naps and nighttime sleep using these methods:

* *Invest in room-darkening or blackout shades because most standard and curtain blinds don't cut out enough light to be effective.* Add them to every window in the room where your child will be learning to sleep and sleeping in the long term.
* *If you're in a temporary living situation or can't invest in blackout shades right now, try a quick fix.* Cover your windows with black garbage bags, taping them up with blue painter's tape (which won't leave marks when removed). Make sure all parts of your window are covered. It'll look dreadful but it works. This garbage bag trick is also great when traveling to visit people who may have not discovered the advantages of an über-dark bedroom. For those who prefer a fancier alternative to the garbage bag, you can buy blackout paper shades that stick to the top of your windowsill. You can cut them to fit perfectly and clip them up during the day to let some light in.
* *If you're sharing a room with your child, this means your bedroom windows will need blackout shades.* The bonus may be that you'll sleep a little better with them up too.

◆ *Already have curtains or blinds, but they don't cut out the sun-light?* It might seem like overkill, but to add that extra level of darkness, we recommend that parents put garbage bags underneath their curtains.

Here's a test to know if the bedtime room is dark enough. Extend your arm straight out in front of you, and wiggle your fingers. You should have a difficult time making out your wiggling fingers. (We confess that it's hard to achieve that level of darkness during daytime naps, but some blackout shades can get it done.)

If you need to interact with your child at night (if he's under four months or you're not starting sleep teaching right now), you may be asking yourself how you'll be able to see to feed, change a diaper, or check on your child. If you need light to tend to your child at night, resist the temptation to keep a night-light or other constant light source on. Instead, put a hall light on and keep the door open while you are in the room. That way, it's a gradual introduction of light rather than a sudden one.

Some parents worry that their children will be afraid of such a dark sleeping space. However, it's very rare for children to develop a fear of darkness until after two years of age. We recommend not using a night-light as long as you can.

Some sneaky sleep stealers may be lurking in your nursery. Most baby monitors, CD players, sound docks, and even humidifiers emit light, which can be very distracting. Turn off the lights in your child's room at night, and see what he sees. Is anything shining into his crib or curtailing your attempts at darkness? If so, identify and fix it. It may be as simple as putting a piece of tape over a little monitor light or turning a CD player around. These little changes can make a big difference.

Add White Noise

Adding white noise to a baby's room is one of the best investments you can make and incredibly helpful at promoting sleep. If possible, we recommend using it from day one, even if you are helping your baby fall asleep. Then use it as long as it's helpful, which for some families with sensitive sleepers or loud households, could be through preschool years.

Here's why we feel so passionately about white noise:

+ *White noise calms very young infants.* The womb is a noisy place. Although white noise doesn't recreate the exact sounds heard inside it, it will help settle newborns. Since they're capable of only lighter stages of sleep, eliminating distractions through a white noise machine can help a baby's sleep from the start.

+ *White noise cuts out ambient noises that may waken your baby.* You won't realize how noisy your home actually is until the moment your baby is asleep. Among the many common culprits are household pets, the doorbell, an air conditioner as it kicks on, a flushing toilet, your neighbor's lawn mower, an ambulance driving down the street, and a toddler who doesn't understand how to get your attention without yelling. The point is that a lot of noises are out of your control and will happen while your baby sleeps. Seize control by adding white noise to dampen the impact of these disruptive noises and make it easier for your child to stay asleep.

+ *White noise can act as a new sleep cue.* Right now, your baby probably associates a certain routine with falling asleep. If this routine requires you to assist with the act of falling asleep, then she's going to be confused when you don't do that "thing" anymore. By turning on white noise every time your baby goes to sleep, she'll soon associate that sound with sleep. If you use white noise from the start, she'll already have some familiarity with what it means when it's time to start sleep teaching. Babies are fast learners, so don't worry if you don't add white noise until the night you start sleep teaching. She'll still catch on quickly that hearing white noise means it's time to sleep.

+ *White noise makes traveling with your baby a breeze.* If you consistently use white noise at home, bring it with you on trips too. When bedtime comes, the new space might look and smell a little different to your baby, but once he hears the familiar sound of white noise, he'll feel a sense of comfort and know it's time to sleep.

Remember that it's never too early, or too late, to add white noise. We suggest introducing it as early as possible so you can start reaping the rewards immediately.

Q: *Won't my baby become addicted to white noise if I use it?*
A: Your child can become accustomed to white noise, but like anything else, you can wean your child off it if you feel it has become problematic. White noise is a tool that makes it easier for your child to sleep more soundly. So to us, worrying that it is a sleep crutch or potentially addicting is like being concerned your child will become addicted to using a sippy cup when she's learning to move away from a bottle. Noise machines make sleep easier, so we encourage you to use this tool to your advantage during sleep teaching. That said, if white noise really concerns you, you can try to phase it out once your child is sleeping better by gradually reducing the volume each day until it's inaudible. However, if as you phase it out you notice your child is waking up more or having difficulty falling asleep, it's probably not the right time to remove it from your sleep routine.

Not all white noise machines are created equal. We know this because we've tested every model on the market we can find. When selecting a white noise machine, make sure it has these two features:

- *No automatic shut-off or permanent timer feature.* You want your white noise machine to stay on the entire time your child is sleeping, day or night.
- *A true white noise option.* Pure white noise is the best setting. However, most sound machines include other sound options like ocean waves, a babbling brook, a heartbeat, and the womb. Although these are soothing sounds, they don't cover up ambient noise as well as true white noise does. They also have variations in the sounds, which can be distracting for very sensitive babies and toddlers.

We recommend that you turn the white noise machine volume up at least halfway and place it on the opposite side of the room from your child. This way, it's not blasting in your baby's ear and more effectively absorbs sounds. If the room has an echo or is on the small side, you might want to turn it down a notch. The ideal range for your child is between fifty-five and sixty-five decibels. As a reference, a refrigerator humming is about forty decibels and a hair dryer is approximately seventy decibels.

You may already feel overloaded by gadgets in the nursery, but white noise is not the place to skimp. Substituting a fan or humidifier instead of using an actual white noise machine isn't a good option. They aren't generally loud enough, and it's also hard to throw a fan or humidifier into your suitcase when it's time to travel with your child.

"The sound machine that you recommended is definitely key. For both of my children, the machine almost serves as a Pavlov's dog in that they hear it and begin to get into sleep mode. And, of course, the loveys. My son has been cuddling the same little lovey since he was three months old and it definitely helps him fall asleep."
—AMY M., MOM TO MARLIE AND CHRISTIAN

Introduce a Lovey

When we work with families, we always recommend that parents choose one thing to give their child while they sleep: an age-appropriate stuffed animal or blanket a baby can use to self-soothe. Many loveys look like a handkerchief-sized blanket with some sort of stuffed animal head securely attached to the corner.

You may be wondering why we are recommending a lovely because we have said not to put anything in crib. This is the one exception to our rule.

You can start using the lovey outside the crib from your baby's first day of life as long as your baby is supervised. A lot of our clients put them near their babies during feedings so they start to associate it with comforting moments. Your baby doesn't have to worship the lovey in order for this to work. Most babies prefer parents to a lovey any day, so don't let your child's lack of outward display of affection for the lovey discourage you. Keep it as a part of happy moments and know you're planting some seeds of affection at the same time.

Be very thoughtful when selecting a lovey for your child's crib. The reason some children suffocate in their sleep is that they become tangled in blankets or submerged in a pillow and aren't physically capable of wiggling out of the position. The human brain is actually wired to prevent suffocation during sleep, thanks to a reflex that detects an increase in carbon dioxide. If there's too much carbon dioxide present, the reflex kicks in and makes us turn our heads or move our body to find oxygen. If your baby is tangled or caught in a certain place, he may not be able to get out despite this involuntary reflex. Make sure the lovey you choose can't wrap entirely around his face or cause a smothering risk. As long as it's lightweight, not too big, is a material that doesn't cut off baby's oxygen, and doesn't have any batting or stuffing, you can be comfortable that it's a safe choice. Also, check that no parts of the lovey can become unattached and pose a choking hazard.

Once your baby reaches four months of age and you're ready to start sleep training, a lovey is ready to take on its new role.

dream team

"At four months, you may introduce a small, safe lovey during sleep times."

—DR. AMY DEMATTIA, PEDIATRICIAN

A lovey is a great sleep tool after the four-month mark because your baby should be developmentally capable of grabbing it and using it to soothe herself. We have the opportunity to watch babies use their loveys in all sorts of ways—chewing it, sucking it, shoving it in their mouths, rubbing it on their faces, snuggling with it. The great thing is your baby will decide how she wants to use it.

Your baby may not fall deeply and madly in love with the lovey right away, but after enough days, weeks, and months together, a bond will form.

Think of this little lovey as a sleep buddy and offer it to your child only during sleep times. Once you move it into the crib after four months, it should essentially leave only for regular washings and travel. Limiting lovey access will make the times your baby has with it feel special and give him something to look forward to when he gets in his crib. Once you see how much love your baby has for his sleep buddy, it'll be tempting to give it to him when he asks for it during the day. Resist the temptation!

If your child is over four months old and doesn't have a lovey yet, don't panic. You can introduce a lovey at any time. Before you give the lovey to your baby, rub it over yourself and your partner. Your baby spends a great deal of time with her face close to you, so your natural scent is very familiar to her. You can put the lovey in your own bed and sleep with it for a few nights and even carry it around during the day to ensure that it picks up your scent. That way, when you present the new sleep buddy to your baby, it'll smell familiar and comforting.

Monitor the Temperature

Talking about the outside temperature is always a safe topic at a dinner party, but as it relates to a baby's bedroom, temperature quickly turns contentious. Fortunately, there is a perfect temperature—and a lot of science to support it. The best temperature for sleeping (for both babies and adults) is between sixty-eight and seventy-two degrees Fahrenheit. If babies sleep in a room that's too warm, their bodies have to work extra hard to cool off. Their sleep will be interrupted, they'll more frequently rouse, and they won't be comfortable. Keeping your baby's room under seventy-two degrees is also an important SIDS preventative measure.

We often encounter resistance from parents who are absolutely certain their baby will be cold without blankets in a room set between sixty-eight and seventy-two degrees. We're cuddly moms and love our extra-warm duvets in the winter, so we understand your desire to bundle up your baby. But your baby doesn't need blankets or sleep sacks or three layers of pajamas.

Here's how to master temperature and keep your baby comfortable:

+ *Purchase a small room thermometer you can put near the crib.* Without a digital thermostat, many parents find it's hard to tell if the room is the right temperature. Some people might think it's hot. Others may say it's chilly. So save yourselves from one more debate. Several baby monitors also display continuous room temperature, which is even better if you're looking to cut down on baby equipment.

+ *Purchase several pairs of footed pajamas.* Even during summer months, keep your child covered up in warm, footed pajamas.

When we're indoors, sixty-eight to seventy-two degrees is the same whether it is summer or winter. We suggest stocking up on different sizes of footed pajamas when they're easy to find in the winter. If you find yourself having to put your baby into a lightweight pair, you can put a onesie underneath. That's truly all the clothing your child will need to stay warm.

- *Your child's hands may feel chilly to you in the morning.* If you notice this, it doesn't mean your baby is too cold or in danger of getting sick. A warm face and chest are better indicators of your baby's comfort. As long as he's dressed in appropriate pajamas and the temperature is sixty-eight degrees or above, he'll be primed for sleep.

- *Warm things up if the rest of your home is cool.* You may deliberately keep your home cooler than sixty-eight degrees at night or are unable to keep the temperature up due to heating issues. In this case, you can layer long-sleeve onesies under thicker-footed pajamas instead of piling extra blankets in your baby's crib, which is unsafe.

"I never knew how much the temperature changed when the door closed at night or how much fluctuation there was. It was eye-opening to see what the temperature really was in my daughter's room and make the appropriate adjustments accordingly. Such a small thing—yet so big!"
—TAMI B., MOM TO ADDISON

Bumper or No Bumper?

Bumpers are controversial among new parents. The American Academy of Pediatrics discourages their use in infants' cribs. According to the recommendation, if a baby lacks the ability to turn his head, bumpers can pose a risk for suffocation or strangulation. That said, some people choose to use bumpers. Here's the rundown on the two sides of this sensitive subject.

Anti-bumpers. Given the safety warnings, it's understandable why many parents opt to go without one. However, without bumpers, babies sometimes knock their hands on the wood rails or get their limbs caught in an opening. Your baby can certainly learn to sleep under these conditions. However, many parents feel distressed when they hear their baby knocking around. Some parents choose a breathable mesh bumper as a middle-ground option. They aren't comfortable but they will keep your baby's arms and legs inside the crib.

Parents who choose not to put a bumper in a crib have these common concerns:

"Oh no! I'm making my child sleep in a wooden box!"
"He misses me and loves cuddling. Now he has nothing to snuggle against."
"Maybe he'd sleep better if I'd put a bumper in his crib."

Pro-bumpers. Most bumpers are made of fabric and add some comfort and softness to your baby's crib. If you feel strongly about having a bumper, choose one with many ties so it can securely attach to a crib. Bumpers should be on the thin side—if you can't part with one, look for something quilted or sparsely stuffed. Any bumper that has so much stuffing it resembles a pillow or engulfs your baby is definitely not a good option.

It should also give when pressed down so it doesn't act as a step when your baby becomes a bit more mobile (and adventurous).

Parents who choose to put a bumper in a crib have these common concerns:

"Oh no! The baby's quiet. I'm worried he isn't breathing! I need to wake him up!"

"I'm here now, but what happens once I go to sleep? How will I
    know if she's stuck in the bumper?"
"I wish I hadn't put that bumper in the crib, but I'm worried whether
    it's fair to take it out now that he's learned to sleep with it."

Try to decide which situation will bother you less. Then try to
stick with the decision you make while you are working on sleep. At
Dream Team Baby, we try to make things as easy as possible for the
baby by making one deal and sticking with it (we'll talk more about
that in later chapters).

Double-Check Crib Height and Location

If you've been in response mode up until now (going to your baby
each time she wakes up), the likelihood that your baby is moving all
over the crib is pretty low. But once you teach your baby to love
sleep, she's going to start expanding her horizons, so make sure you
drop the crib mattress to a safe height. Many parents forget to do
this and are surprised when their baby starts sitting up or pulling
to a standing position. Our children grow up in the blink of an eye,
even when we are not hovering over them, so try to lower the mattress before you start sleep teaching. This way, you are ready for your
baby's next milestone.

To determine the safest crib height, assume your child is going
to hit that next major physical milestone each time you put him in
a crib. If he's rolling over, make sure the crib is at a height appropriate
for a baby who is sitting up. If your baby is sitting up, make sure
your crib is at a height appropriate for a baby who is standing up.

Where the crib is positioned in a room is also important for
sleep. Some parents put the crib directly under a heating or cooling
vent. It can be pretty bothersome to awaken to a blast of cool or hot
air several times a night.

Here are a few other things to take into consideration when
deciding where to place your baby's crib:

+ Don't put the crib underneath a window.
+ Pay attention to anything that might be within your baby's grasp.
+ Do not hang heavy objects or shelving directly above your child's crib.

If Sharing a Room, Carve Out a Separate Sleeping Space for Your Baby

Due to space constraints, plenty of parents need to share a room with their child or would like their baby to share a room with a sibling. This is possible, but it's much easier if you can create some sort of physical separation between your baby and you or his siblings during sleep times. Many babies have trouble going back to sleep if they can see you lying a few feet away.

The easiest option is putting a screen up. But many parents are worried about having something in the room that can topple over if a child bumps into it. Our favorite option is a full-length curtain on a cable track similar to what's used in most hospitals (more attractive, of course!). You can always use a free-standing screen, but with a track system, you won't have to worry about anything falling over, and during the day, a curtain can easily be pulled back to open up the room again. The same setup can be applied for siblings who share a room.

A barrier in a room is a good way to add a feeling of privacy and cut out the distractions in a room, but it doesn't entirely cut out the disruptions that come when sharing a room with another person. Even if you have a screen or curtain, you'll want to give your baby a separate space when teaching him to sleep. That means separating children temporarily during the learning process or moving yourselves out into the living room for a few days.

Sweet Dreams!

We can't tell you how many times we say, "Clear the clutter," and parents disregard the advice because they love the baby's mobile so much. Or we say, "Darken the room," and parents ignore that advice or skip putting up the garbage bags because of how it might look to neighbors. Later in the book, we make other suggestions that are much harder to do than these cosmetic changes. But if you force yourself to follow through on the easy stuff, it'll make things that much easier for your baby to learn. Remember that the harder the lesson is for your baby, the more frustrated your baby will get. If you want your baby to learn the easiest way possible, do yourself and your baby a favor and stick with our advice. You'll be glad you did.

Transitioning from Adulthood to
Parenthood and Facing Adversity

DIANA AND SCOTT K., PARENTS OF LEO AND AIDAN

Even after our first baby's open-heart surgery, being carefree was a
total fit for our lives. See, being a control freak attached to a schedule and plan doesn't really work when your baby has a 1 percent
chance of living.

After his surgeries, our son was more or less a two-hour sleeper,
and we felt that's just who he is and we should just accept that and
be grateful for another day with him. We spent a lot of time in
survival mode. Scott went back to work, and other moms made me
feel resentful when I heard them complaining about things like colic.

In hindsight, I wasn't angry at them; I was just angry at all we had been through.

It took me a full year to get to a point where I reached out for help. I didn't feel that I had the right to ask for help—not when my child survived when other families we met at the hospital had lost theirs. That was a huge mistake. Both Scott and I felt we were just victims of circumstance, and the fact that our sons weren't good sleepers was something we had just accepted.

My aha! moment was understanding that what happens during the day is a direct reflection on what will happen at night. It really was WOW! So we keep to the daytime schedule no matter how difficult it is for me, my husband, and even family and friends to accept. I could list things like the sound machine, the trash bags, but none of it was more life-changing for us than the realization that who we are being during the day with our children is going to directly bear on the level of ease and grace during their bedtime routine.

I now coach all my intense mommy friends around accepting that life does need to change if you want your day to go smoothly. I spent so much time trying to be who I used to be before children, and after three years of failing, I finally accepted that I have a choice to continue the way I was going or let it go and accept that there's another life in my life and to make this work for everyone.

By the time we finally started sleep teaching, Leo was three-and-a-half years old and starting to have some behavioral issues—telling us how, when, and where he would sleep. Now he's so sweet, so well adjusted, and so good. I'm not sure that would've happened if we hadn't made the decision to sleep-teach.

I feel that anyone reading this book is going to read this story of ours and think, "If they could do this, anyone can!" and I hope they do. The biggest gift of all is that we have our lives back. We're sane and healthy again.

CHAPTER 4

Identifying Your Child's Sleep Associations

The next step to creating a dream sleeper is developing a deeper understanding of the things your baby currently requires to fall asleep—in other words, her sleep associations. As we discussed in Chapter Two, a sleep association is anything, positive or negative, that your baby associates with the act of falling asleep. Until four months of age, you needn't worry about your baby's sleep associations, but after four months, children are ready to shed their negative sleep associations and learn more positive, sustainable, and healthy ones.

Keys to Zzzs

- **Know your role in your baby's sleep associations.** You contribute a lot more than you think to her positive and negative habits.
- **Make a list of your child's negative sleep associations.** Understanding them is the key to fixing them.
- **Stay focused on progress.** Once you phase out negative associations, try not to lapse back into them.

A positive sleep association is something that an individual has control over—for example:

+ Thumb sucking
+ Rhythmic behavior such as rubbing one's face or one's feet or moving one's head
+ Lying in a particular position—on one's side, front, or back

A positive sleep association can also take the form of something that is a constant variable during sleep, such as a white noise machine or a dark room.

A negative sleep association is something over which an individual does *not* have control—for example:

+ Falling asleep while nursing or taking a bottle
+ Being rocked
+ Body contact with a parent or other caregiver
+ Being bounced
+ Moving in a swing
+ Being swaddled
+ Sucking on a pacifier (under six months or so)
+ Having a completely full stomach

If you did all of the things we have listed to get your baby to sleep last night, don't feel bad. They're normal techniques we all use to soothe our children when they enter this world. They become a problem only when we keep doing these techniques long after our children need us to (even if they would still like us to do these things). Most parents don't adapt their routine as quickly as their babies grow, so there's usually a period when parents are doing something for their baby that the baby can do on his or her own. This situation is complicated by the fact that babies aren't fully aware of how capable they are. A baby who is rocked or fed to sleep thinks that's the way sleep should be. Sleep teaching is really just about clarifying the misunderstanding.

The Pacifier: Friend or Foe?

Let's talk about the beloved (and loathed) pacifier and how it relates to sleep. In our experience, it is best to take away the pacifier when sleep teaching begins. Many parents have more of an emotional attachment to pacifiers than their children actually do and are stunned when their baby forgets about it after a day or two. The pacifier is a hot-button issue with parents who have used it successfully because they see how much their baby loves it. However, most babies under six months don't have the fine motor skills required to put a pacifier back in their mouths when it falls out. So it isn't fair if you offer it in the beginning of the night if it isn't going to be there in the middle of the night. Babies over six months may have the ability to get a pacifier back in their mouths, but whenever they need it in the night, it can turn into an all-out adrenaline-inducing manhunt. If your baby has to crawl around to search for the pacifier, she will be wide awake, and it can be harder for her to put herself back to sleep. Sure, you can combat the searching by adding lots of pacifiers to the crib, but then you are making the crib a pacifier mine field, not the most comfortable environment. Bottom line: it's almost always in everyone's best interest to make a clean break with the pacifier when you are ready to sleep-teach.

When you're ready to start working on sleep, it's a good idea to write down whatever your child needs to fall asleep, for naps and for bedtime. What parts of the routine involve you, your partner, or your caregivers?

My Child's Sleep Associations

_____
_____
_____
_____
_____

Take a good look at this list, because it's all about to change! In Part Three, we'll help you usher in some positive associations to replace these negative ones.

In essence, teaching your baby to be an independent sleeper is the process of removing all of your child's negative sleep associations. If you feel that you are not ready to remove the negative associations you listed, you are probably not ready for sleep teaching. When parents try sleep teaching but don't phase out all sleep associations (for example, feeding your baby at night long after you know the feeding is not for nutrition), it's working against the grain. If you continue to help your baby, she will continue to need you to respond when she rouses. This usually leads to parents giving up on sleep training because their baby doesn't show progress.

For example, if you do everything we suggest but continue to replace a pacifier in the middle of the night when you hear your baby rouse, you are still participating in the falling-asleep process. If you're participating in the falling-asleep process, you're setting your baby up to fail. If you can't bear the thought of not giving a pacifier back in the middle of the night, or not nursing or holding your baby

When to Stop Swaddling

The optimal time to stop swaddling is between two months and four months of age. By the time babies reach four months, they will benefit from the freedom to move at night. It may not be something they immediately embrace, but all that nighttime movement helps their gross motor development. This is crucial for upcoming milestones like crawling, standing, and walking.

Never try to teach your baby to sleep while swaddled. It inhibits their self-soothing ability and makes it harder for a baby to learn.

until she falls asleep, you shouldn't start sleep teaching yet. Following some of our other suggestions (environment, schedule, feedings, which we will cover in the next few chapters) should help improve your current sleep situation. However, you may not achieve eleven to twelve hours of uninterrupted nighttime sleep until you've dealt with sleep associations.

The other reason we recommend identifying and taking the time to write down all of your baby's negative sleep associations is that down the road, long after sleep training is over, your baby is bound to have a rough night. Maybe he'll be sick. Maybe he'll be out of sorts because he skipped a few naps while you were having a great time on vacation. Whatever the reason, you'll most likely return to interacting with your child at night on a temporary basis. That's okay, but whatever you do, try not to fall back on one of your child's old sleep associations. If your baby used to sleep in your bed, plan to do anything except bring him back into the bed if he's sick or having a hard night. It's even okay to bring your baby into the living room and watch a baby video for thirty minutes in the night if he truly needs you, but if your baby used to fall asleep on you, do anything but resorting to the old modus operandi.

There's a good reason we're telling you all of these things. There's a great scene in the movie *Dumb and Dumber* where Lauren Holly tells Jim Carrey that there's a 1 in 1 million chance she'd ever date him. Instead of feeling rejected, Carrey responds, "So you're telling me there's a chance?" This is how your child can feel if he sees a glimmer of opportunity—and that 1 in 1 million chance makes it that much harder for your baby to get back on track once things return to normal.

"Having read everything and tried all kinds of advice, our six month old was still waking every two to three hours to feed! A light bulb moment for us was understanding that we had essentially trained him to sleep only on a completely full stomach. Our son would digest a little, and if

he roused at all, he'd holler to be fed. Once we got him on solids, so we would not worry he was super hungry, we forged ahead and within two weeks, he was sleeping eleven and a half hours consistently!"
—SHELLEY AND WEST H., PARENTS OF DASH

Sweet Dreams!

Though the aim of this book is teaching your child healthy sleeping patterns, it's crucial to keep his or her sleep associations in mind so you can address each one in an organized, gradual manner. You can't move forward until you know exactly which direction you're going in, and your map of your child's sleep associations will help you navigate the rough spots or reorient you should you become lost on the road ahead.

First-Time Parents Trying to Keep Afloat

SALLY AND MARK S., PARENTS OF ALESSANDRA

When we started working on sleep, our baby was five and a half months old and had never slept longer than two hours in a row in her life. Frankly, since her birth, neither had we. We must have been some of the most exhausted and desperate parents who have ever called asking for help.

Mark and I aren't sure how we ended up in such bad shape. We had read every book there was, but the only way to get her to sleep was to nurse her or walk her around in her stroller or walk around with her in our baby carrier. We'd do laps around our apartment since constant motion was necessary. We moved to a two-bedroom apartment when she was a little older, and the carpet from our old apartment, where we had lived for five years before we had her, literally had a circle track on it!

She'd usually sleep for thirty minutes, or two hours at the longest. So we finally resorted to letting her sleep in our bed, which, as I think back on it now, was just hideous, but we were desperate and tired. Basically every thirty minutes, all night long, she would nurse. We made many mistakes, but at the time, we honestly thought we were doing the right things.

My husband is the one who actually called for help. He said half-jokingly, "Either I'm going to have to institutionalize you, or we're going to need some help, Sally. You can't live like this." It wasn't healthy for any of us.

Our advice is: Don't wait five months—things can be better!

People think we're nuts and maybe we are, but we have a child who sleeps now and until very recently (she's now twenty-six months) had never skipped a nap. We have double blackout shades. We keep the room cold. We don't go anywhere without our noise machine and some black trash bags.

Dream Team kept telling us to believe in Alessandra and assured us that she could do it. They told us to stick with Alessandra's new schedule, and we did.

Alessandra went from being a crabby, screaming child to a delightful little girl—and we know sleep has everything to do with it.

CHAPTER 5

Creating a Daytime Sleeping and Eating Schedule

Children under the age of two have very little choice in their lives. They follow our lead, wear the clothes we choose (most of the time, anyway), and eat what we're serving for dinner. On some level, we can all understand that lack of choice can be a little frustrating. However, for children, it's actually very reassuring, not restricting, to have a predictable pattern to each day. With a schedule, children know what to expect, and this makes them feel safe and comforted.

Keys to Zzzs

- **Identify the best daytime nap schedule.** If you're not ready to move to sleep teaching yet, it's still helpful to follow a general nap schedule. Even if your baby still relies on you to fall asleep at naptime, getting his body used to a schedule will help him work toward getting the sleep he needs. We've provided some age-appropriate schedules in this chapter.

- **Pick a bedtime, and then stick to it.** An ideal bedtime for children from eight weeks to six or seven years of age is between

6:00 P.M. and 8:00 P.M. Keep in mind that not all babies under four months will be able to stick to it every night, but some will. We have provided several schedule choices for you in this chapter. Use the bedtime you chose for your baby to select the best schedule for you.

- *If you're not sleep teaching,* feel free to start your schedule whenever you're ready. However, don't follow the schedule too rigidly. Until a baby is getting solid nights of sleep without interruption, her daytime sleep needs constant change.

- *If you know you're moving on to sleep teaching right away,* wait to introduce a schedule until after the first night of sleep teaching. This is extremely important, and we'll explain why in Part Three. After you've established your schedule, try to stick to it as closely as possible. Pushing a nap or bedtime back by only fifteen minutes can be difficult or confusing for some children.

The Art of the Schedule

Many new parents we talk to feel overwhelmed by routine and schedule. Sometimes it's the spontaneity—whether it's an impulsive walk around the block or coffee with friends while your baby sleeps in the stroller—that gives some parents a little taste of their old life.

So when we recommend schedules, we can be met with understandable trepidation and downright refusal as parents think, *What is life going to feel like if those little bits of joy are taken away?* Of course, those little bits of joy are going to be replaced by other types of joy, but we know that sometimes people rebel against the schedule because they are afraid of the unknown.

"Some parents are reluctant to give up their freedom by adopting a sleep schedule. It's hard to change if you're a fly-by-the-seat-of-your-pants sort of person. To these parents I say, 'I know scheduling doesn't fit into your vision of your life as a parent, but neither do sleepless nights. It's time to try a new way if you want to solve a problem.'"

—DR. INGRID SCHWEIGER, PSYCHOTHERAPIST

The schedules we offer in this chapter will be a positive force in your life when you're ready. And even if your baby is too young to put on a schedule, keep these universal principles in mind as you create a game plan for your day.

Feedings

You'll notice we encourage you to feed your baby when he wakes up from a nap instead of right before he goes down for a nap. Eating when he wakes up ensures he isn't eating too close to a naptime. Nursing or sucking on a bottle can result in instant baby narcolepsy, which is a great thing when you just want your baby to sleep, but it can also teach babies that they always need a completely full stomach to fall asleep.

Naptime

Naps should occur at regular intervals during the day, equally spaced so there's plenty of time for the holy grail of childhood: playtime. We also encourage parents to wake children up from afternoon naps after two and a half hours. Any longer and bedtime could become a battle.

Choosing a Bedtime

In general, children over four months of age should be awake for the two and a half to four hours leading up to bedtime (awake time gets longer as the child gets older). It's helpful to preserve this last awake period of the day so children are tired enough at bedtime to sleep for an extended period of time at night (ideally twelve hours).

Creating the Ideal Bedtime Routine

You've probably heard that having a predictable bedtime routine is a helpful way to tell your baby the day is ending. That's true. When you put her pajamas on and cue her favorite wind-down music, you trigger in your baby's mind the rest of the steps before bedtime. But this is an area where you don't need to stress out and overcomplicate things. Your baby isn't going to sleep better because you've created an elaborate, "om-inducing" bedtime routine. Here's something that may surprise you: the best bedtime routine may not involve low lights, soft music, and quiet cuddling. It may involve tickle time with one or both parents and stacking blocks. The most important thing you can do is make the final moments before bed a sacred, pleasant time. Yes, the bedtime routine is a signal that sleep time is coming, but it isn't supposed to get your child almost asleep. We'll talk about this more in the coming chapters.

Anyone who has a child knows it's virtually impossible to recreate the same calming, predictable routine single day. Sometimes Daddy or Mommy comes home late from work or Grandma calls to say hi to the kids just before bed.

So instead of going against the grain, work with it. Replace the word *calming* in your mind with *intimate*. Think of your child's bedtime routine as a moment in your day when you stop chores and focus on being present and connecting with your children. Ignore the bills and e-mails, and don't worry about getting the kids too excited before bed.

That said, if you and your baby enjoy quiet time yourselves, go ahead and do some of that baby massage. Just don't feel that you have to massage every night or that bedtime will be completely thrown off if your daughter is more interested in something else one night. Move on, read books instead, and don't force the issue. It's more important that the last two minutes before bedtime stay the same than the entire fifteen to twenty minutes of the bedtime routine.

Here's an example of a good bedtime routine:

1. Put on pajamas.
2. Have some together time: playing, tickling, reading books, singing songs, massaging, or cuddling, for example, or some combination of these.

3. Brush your child's teeth (if she has any yet!).
4. Goodnight kisses to everyone in the house.
5. Change your baby's diaper.
6. Turn on the white noise in your baby's room, and turn off the light.
7. Kiss your baby good night, and put him in crib.

> Even if you help your child fall asleep at naptime or if your child naturally falls asleep on her own, the best naps occur in your child's sleep space. If you've followed our advice about setting up your sleep space, it's a controlled environment primed for sleep.

Daytime Sleep Schedules for Parents Not Moving On to Part Three Immediately

If you are not ready to start working on sleep teaching, following a somewhat consistent sleep schedule (one that is age appropriate) may be enough to help your baby's sleep improve. However, we don't advise rigid adherence to a schedule if your nighttime still includes a lot of waking up and varying start times to the day. If you are not doing all the pieces of our approach, getting your baby on an exact schedule may be an uphill battle. In fact, trying to do so could push any sane parent over the edge. For example, if you've just gotten your baby to fall back asleep at 6:30 A.M. after ninety minutes of rocking and nursing, it's going to be painful to wake her up at 7:00 A.M. just because it's a designated wake-up time according to your schedule. If you are not moving on to Part Three, the schedules included in this chapter should act as a guide rather than a playbook.

Until sleep teaching begins, it's best not to overexpect from your baby. There will be days when your baby conks out in the stroller out of the blue, falls asleep too early, or sleeps only twenty minutes for a nap that is usually an hour. When that happens, don't sweat it. Even just trying to stay on a sleep schedule is a step in the right direction. And seeing your child's progress may encourage you to move on to sleep teaching.

For those of you who struggle to stick to a bedtime each day, don't get discouraged. There's still hope for your angel. We call these babies *sensitive sleepers*, which means that sleep won't come together until you fix everything in Part Three. In these cases, your best option is to surrender to chaos until you are ready to put the whole picture together.

Sleep Schedules

Sleep schedules are one of the most critical components of sleep teaching plans, and they vary depending on your baby's age. That's why we suggest making modifications as you go.

Schedule for a Two to Four Month Old

Between eight and sixteen weeks, your baby can start to follow a daytime schedule as long as you don't adhere too rigidly to it. Remember that each child is different, so use our advice as a loose guide. Even if your baby's daytime sleep is still a bit unpredictable, it's a good first step to have a set bedtime at this age. If you're able to start structuring sleep this way before your baby is four months old, you are laying important groundwork for her to learn how to sleep through the night once she's a little older.

Don't feel that there's something wrong if your baby doesn't conform to a schedule at this age. If your child is colicky or experiencing gastrointestinal issues or reflux, he may be more difficult to settle and have a hard time sleeping in longer stretches. Even if you have a child without issues, he may not sleep for more than forty-five minutes at naptime, and that's okay. It's developmentally normal. He should start to get better at napping as he approaches the four-month mark.

If you start a schedule before sixteen weeks and find it's an uphill battle, don't worry about it. As we said, there's no way to make any sleep mistakes the first few months. Think of starting a schedule early as extra credit—a nice-to-do, but not a need-to-do. You can always stop and pick it up later if it isn't working.

As you review the schedule in Table 5.1 for your two to four month old, keep these two points in mind:

- An asterisk in this and the other tables in this chapter means your baby can sleep an additional thirty minutes if she's still asleep at the wake-up time. This extra time helps children get more sleep when they're extra tired, but not so much sleep that their nighttime sleep is compromised.
- Most babies at this stage are not sleeping uninterrupted at night. If you have a lot of activity at night, your baby may need longer naps during the day.

It's never too late to introduce a schedule. Your child never ages out at a chance to be good sleeper.

Following this schedule is a great first step to helping your baby organize sleep throughout the day. In later schedules you will see that we recommend putting your baby in bed awake for sleeping times, but you certainly do not need to do that at this stage of your baby's life.

Time	Activity
Table 5.1 Daily Schedule for a Two to Four Month Old	
Time	Activity
7:00 A.M.*	Wake and milk feeding
7:30–9:00 A.M.	Playtime!
9:00 A.M.	Nap #1
10:00 A.M.*	Wake and milk feeding
10:30 A.M.–12:00 P.M.	Playtime!
12:00 P.M.	Nap #2
1:00 P.M.*	Wake and milk feeding
1:30–3:00 P.M.	Playtime!
3:00 P.M.	Nap #3
4:00 P.M.*	Wake and milk feeding
4:30–6:00 P.M.	Playtime!
5:00 P.M.	Optional nap (about 20 to 30 minutes)
7:00–8:00 P.M.	Milk feeding (not fed in nursery) and bedtime
Nighttime sleep	One to three nighttime feeds depending on child

*Optional thirty minutes of bonus sleep.

Schedule for Children Four Months and Older

Once your baby reaches sixteen weeks, his stomach is large enough to consume enough food during the day so he can go eleven or twelve hours through the night without a feeding. This may require transferring feedings from nighttime to daytime to keep his overall intake constant. Since he's still growing so much, he'll need to nap approximately two to four and a half hours a day. These naps will usually range from forty-five to ninety minutes each and occur one and a half to two hours apart.

Obviously children aren't robots, so on some days, they're going to have different sleep needs. Therefore, we build bonus time into the schedules to allow for such variations. The important thing is that if your baby does take the bonus sleep, the rest of the schedule does not change. That way, she's on a rhythm, and her body can start to predict when sleeping times are coming.

The tables that follow are some examples of an ideal schedule for a child on a 7:00 A.M. to 7:00 P.M. schedule. You may be shocked by these schedules if your baby is not sleeping anywhere near this amount of time. He can get there! But if your baby's not yet four months or you're not ready to start training because of a trip coming up, or visitors coming, or simply because you aren't emotionally ready to ask your baby to sleep by himself, these schedules can still help you. Even if you still need to help your baby fall asleep, you can keep helping him fall back asleep until the scheduled wake-up time. That way, he'll have established a rhythm by the time you begin training.

As you review the schedules in the tables, keep these points in mind:

+ An asterisk in the tables means your baby can sleep an additional thirty minutes if she's still asleep at the wake-up time. This extra time helps children get more sleep when they're extra tired, but not so much sleep that their nighttime sleep is compromised.

+ The average nap cycle is approximately forty-five minutes. When children have long naps (ninety minutes), they usually cycle through two nap cycles. Some children wake up between these cycles, but if they are given a chance (that is, you don't run to them the minute they cry), they can learn to fall back asleep and get the sleep they need.

+ If you're planning to sleep-teach, we'll get into how to encourage your child to take longer naps and sleep longer intervals at night in the next few chapters. If you're not planning to sleep-teach, then how you help your child get the naps she needs is up to you.

+ Even if you decide not to use our sleep teaching plan in Part Three, these schedules can still help.

Q: *Should we wake a sleeping baby if a nap is going too long?*

A: Yes and no. If you are trying to help your baby sleep longer and better at night and he is over four months old, we do recommend waking your baby from naps, unless he's sick. However, if your baby is under four months, we generally do not recommend waking him unless it's the final nap before bedtime. Waking your baby will ensure he's properly tired when it's time to go to sleep for the night. So if bedtime is 7:30 P.M., try to wake him up from his nap by 5:30 P.M.

Table 5.2   Daily Schedule for a Four to Six Month Old Who Is Not Eating Solids

Time	Activity
7:00 A.M.*	Wake and milk feeding
7:30–9:00 A.M.	Playtime!
9:00 A.M.	Nap #1 (put in crib awake)
10:00 A.M.*	Wake and milk feeding
10:30 A.M.–12:00 P.M.	Playtime!
12:00 P.M.	Nap #2 (put in crib awake)
1:00 P.M.*	Wake and milk feeding
1:30–3:00 P.M.	Playtime!
3:00 P.M.	Nap #3 (put in crib awake)
4:00 P.M.*	Wake and milk feeding
4:30–6:00 P.M.	Playtime!
6:15 P.M.	Bathed and dressed for bed
6:30 P.M.	Milk feeding, not fed in nursery
6:50 P.M.	Bedtime routine (book, song)
7:00 P.M.	Bedtime (put in crib awake)

*Optional thirty minutes of bonus sleep.

Table 5.3   Daily Schedule for a Four to Six Month Old Who Is Eating Solids

Time	Activity
7:00 A.M.*	Wake and milk feeding
8:00 A.M.	Breakfast
9:00 A.M.	Nap #1 (put in crib awake)
10:00 A.M.*	Wake and milk feeding
10:30–11:30 A.M.	Playtime!
11:30 A.M.	Lunch
12:00 P.M.*	Nap #2 (put in crib awake)
1:00 P.M.	Wake and milk feeding
3:00 P.M.	Nap #3 (put in crib awake)
4:00 P.M.*	Wake and milk feeding
4:30–5:45 P.M.	Playtime!
5:45 P.M.	Dinner
6:15 P.M.	Bathed and dressed for bed
6:30 P.M.	Milk feeding, not fed in nursery
6:50 P.M.	Bedtime routine (book, song)
7:00 P.M.	Bedtime (put in crib awake)

*Optional thirty minutes of bonus sleep.

Table 5.4 Daily Schedule for a Six to Fifteen Month Old	
Time	Activity
7:00 A.M.*	Wake and milk feeding
8:00 A.M.	Breakfast
9:00 A.M.	Nap #1 (put in crib awake)
10:00 A.M.*	Wake and milk feeding
10:30 A.M.–12:00 P.M.	Playtime
12:00 P.M.	Lunch
1:00 P.M.	Nap #2 (put in crib awake)
3:00 P.M.	Wake and milk feeding
3:30–5:30 P.M.	Playtime!
5:45 P.M.	Dinner
6:15 P.M.	Bathed and dressed for bed
6:30 P.M.	Milk feeding, not fed in nursery
6:45 P.M.	Bedtime routine (book, song)
7:00 P.M.	Bedtime (put in crib awake)

*Optional thirty minutes of bonus sleep.

Table 5.5 Daily Schedule for a Fifteen Month to Three Year Old

Time	Activity
7:00 A.M.*	Wake and milk feeding
8:00 A.M.	Breakfast
8:30–10:30 A.M.	Playtime!
10:30 A.M.	Light snack
12:30 P.M.	Lunch
1:00–3:00 P.M.*	Nap (put in crib awake)
3:00 P.M.	Milk feeding
3:30 P.M.	Playtime!
4:00 P.M.	Light snack
5:30 P.M.	Dinner with milk
6:15 P.M.	Bathed and dressed for bed
6:30 P.M.	Optional milk feeding
6:50 P.M.	Bedtime routine (book, song)
7:00 P.M.	Bedtime (put in crib awake)

*Optional thirty minutes of bonus sleep.

Playtime Is Important Too!

You'll see playtime scheduled several times throughout your child's day. We know this may seem obvious, but we're including it here because it's so important to stimulate your baby. Sometimes it's easy to forget to play when you're exhausted. Especially for second children, it's easy for their awake time to be filled with trips to the grocery store and sitting in an exerciser while you fold clothes or make dinner. We don't mean you need to spend every waking moment playing with your child, but do keep it in mind.

There are many benefits of play. First, it'll help tire out your baby, so he'll go to bed more easily. Second, fresh air and sunlight offer important emotional benefits for all of us, including your baby. And on a deeper level, play is your baby's work—it's how she learns. Until your baby's brain is mature enough to have more internal play like pretend and imagination, she'll rely on you to help facilitate playtime.

"Learning about sleep as a twenty-four-hour process that's influenced by eating, napping, and activity throughout the day helped us realize how many factors influence sleep. Being armed with a set schedule and a plan that addressed all of the if-then situations we were troubled by was incredibly valuable."
—JEN B., MOM TO EITAN

Sweet Dreams!

When children have a regular cadence to their day, they know what to expect, which is comforting to them and helps them feel emotionally secure. By learning to follow a schedule, they can relax into their day and focus on more important things—like trying to roll across the room.

CHAPTER 6

Fixing Potential Feeding Issues

You've got your baby's room set up, you've identified your child's negative sleep associations, and you've put together a schedule for your child. Now it's time to look at your child's daily nutrition to make sure dietary issues are not preventing her from sleeping. Many times feeding changes can improve sleep without even making any changes at night.

Keys to Zzzs

- **Keep feeding logs.** That way, you'll get your baby's full eating and sleeping picture.

- **Get a baseline for your baby's typical food intake over twenty-four hours.** This will give you a good idea of what to expect on most days.

- **Maximize daytime breast milk or formula intake.** Keeping your baby full will naturally help her to sleep better.

- **Keep him interested in eating.** Introduce solid food into your child's diet carefully.

Keeping Logs

When you are an overly tired parent, days blur into nights. It can be hard to remember what happened this morning, much less yesterday. Taking a few days of detailed logs will allow you to see on paper what's actually going on and identify any patterns that exist. Many parents have aha! moments when they review a few days of logs. For example, they may see that their child is eating every sixty minutes toward the end of the day, which will lead them to ask whether she is crying because she's tired or because she is truly hungry.

Having a log of how much your child eats in a typical twenty-four-hour period will also give you a benchmark for what's typical for him. When you have an intake baseline (such as twenty-eight ounces of milk), you have a daytime goal to aim for. This is particularly helpful if you are concerned your child will be hungry at night. If you are able to get your baby to eat close to his normal twenty-four-hour amount between waking up and bedtime, then you can be more assured that he doesn't need to eat at night. Sure, he may be used to eating at night, but with some encouragement, he should be able to make it through the night without a nighttime feed.

Figure 6.1 shows an example of a log a client filled out before we started working with her family. You'll use logs like this to help with the rest of your assignments in this chapter. Copy the one in Appendix C or download it from our Web site at www.dreamteambaby.com.

Maximizing Your Feedings

Nutrition is always a major concern of ours before we ask a baby to start sleeping through the night. Some parents are surprised we spend so much time discussing it, since they called us for sleep help. Once parents learn how to get the most out of daytime feedings, nighttime teaching is easier.

Figure 6.1   Sample Log

Date: August 5

Time	Activity (i.e., sleeping, eating, fussing)	Notes
7:30 am	Woke up and nursed	
9:00 am	2 oz. cereal + 1 oz. prunes	
10:00 am	Acting tired, refused breast	
11:00–11:45 am	Nap in stroller	Woke up when ambulance drove by
2:30 pm	Bottle (breast milk, 4 oz.)	
3:45–5:00 pm	Nap in crib	
5:30 pm	Bottle (breast milk, 4 oz.)	Still seemed hungry, but refused additional bottle
6:45–7:15 pm	Nap in stroller	
7:15 pm	2 oz. sweet potatoes + 1 oz. green beans	
8:45 pm	Bath	
9:15 pm	Bottle (formula, 5 oz.)	
12:30 am	Woke-up	Cried, replaced paci, fell asleep in 10 minutes
2:30 am	Woke-up	Nursed 4 minutes
4:30 am	Woke-up	Let cry 5 minutes, then nursed 2 minutes

Babies Three to Six Months Old

Many parents think the best way to help their baby increase the ounces of milk she takes during the day is to let her eat frequently. This is actually not true. Another misconception many parents have is that their baby is starving because she seems insatiable. Both of these ideas (that babies to need to eat more frequently during the day and that babies are not getting enough milk throughout the day) can undermine a parent's best intentions to take away night feedings once their baby is over four months gestationally.

Laying the proper foundation for nutrition during the daytime can help you know for sure that your baby is getting enough to eat.

So your first assignment is to look at your logs and see if your milk feedings are happening at three- to four-hour intervals.

It doesn't matter whether your baby is on formula or breast milk; it's a myth that exclusively breast-fed babies can't sleep through the night as well as formula-fed babies do. While it's true that breast milk is easier for the baby to digest (a good thing), formula and breast milk actually have the same number of calories (twenty calories per ounce). The biggest difference between the two is how fat is distributed throughout a feeding in a breast-feeding versus formula-fed baby. Understanding the difference will help explain why we care so much about getting the feedings under control before sleep teaching.

There are two kinds of breast milk: foremilk and hindmilk. Foremilk has a greater concentration of water, and hindmilk has a greater concentration of fat. As a baby nurses, he gets the foremilk first, and then he can access the satiating hindmilk to finish the feeding. If your baby isn't hungry enough at a feeding (which happens when feedings are not separated enough), he may not be able to consume enough of the foremilk to get to the hindmilk. Breast-fed babies who eat very frequently might be hydrated but not truly full because they aren't getting the fat that is so satiating. The only way to ensure that the baby is full is by extending the time between feedings so your baby can get to the hindmilk.

Physiologically, feeding is also more effective if the feedings are spaced properly. If you apply conventional dieting wisdom to your baby's eating habits, both formula-fed and breast-fed babies are at a disadvantage if feedings are too close. Adults who are dieting are encouraged to eat smaller portions many times throughout the day to diminish their tendency to overeat at a meal. So, in the same way, if you're feeding your baby small meals throughout the day, she's never truly motivated to take a full feeding because she knows all she has to do is root or cry and she's offered another ounce or two.

Also, when feedings aren't properly spread out, many babies have a hard time differentiating the various cues their body is sending them. If he's always fed when he also happens to be tired, a baby might truly believe he needs to eat when he's feeling sleepy (our supertired babies can seem superhungry). This confusion can also undermine a mother's breast-feeding goals, since she may start to worry that her supply is low.

It's a vicious cycle until you start focusing on extending the feedings. Sometimes it takes a few days to spread out daytime feedings, and it's fine to take your time. For instance, if your baby really is eating every hour during the day, then you may be successful only in extending one feeding interval to three hours. Remember, though, that progress is progress, no matter how small. Most babies catch on within two or three days.

If you're a breast-feeding mom who can't seem to extend feedings, try feeding your baby some expressed breast milk. If you're more successful in extending feedings when your baby is offered a few six-ounce bottles of breast milk, it could be an indicator that there is a problem with the breast feeding. You might need a latch adjustment (a correction in how your baby's attaching to your nipples), you might need to start pumping to increase supply, or you might try augmenting your breast feeding with a bottle of formula. Whatever the case, you should address this with your pediatrician or lactation consultant before you start working on sleep.

If you were able to extend feedings without any problems, you can be confident your baby's ready for the next step!

Our advice to space out and schedule feedings may feel a little uncomfortable to parents who are feeding on demand. There's nothing wrong with feeding on demand, but it's hard to fix sleep without scheduling the feedings. You can't be absolutely certain your baby is getting enough to eat during the day. However, if you do want to start sleep teaching in Part Three, don't ignore our feeding advice.

Successful Breast Feeding and Sleep

by Carolyn Migliore, R.N.

Many mothers worry their babies are not getting enough breast milk, and if their baby is not sleeping well, they tend to think it's because of diminished milk supply. We know that's not always the case. It's very important to instill confidence in mothers who are exclusively breast feeding that they are in fact nourishing their baby adequately.

Following these tips will help give breast-feeding moms peace of mind that they're able to supply their baby all they need to thrive and sleep well:

- *Be comfortable and relaxed during feedings.* This helps foster bonding and makes babies more comfortable, which helps them eat longer.

- *Make sure your baby is awake and alert during feedings.* This will help ensure your child is feeding correctly and has enough stamina to eat until satisfied.

- *Use appropriate positioning during feedings, especially during the first few weeks when babies are so small and still getting the hang of things.* The rule of thumb is this: the baby comes to the breast; the breast doesn't come to the baby. Babies should also face the breast, which is easiest to do in the cross-cradle, football, and side-lying positions.

- *Pay close attention to latching.* If babies are not latched correctly, they can't adequately empty a breast and therefore have an inadequate feed. This will cause them to want to feed more often and likely wake up more during the night since they were not fed adequately during the day.

- *Be mindful of maternal nutrition and hydration.* Early on in breast feeding, mothers are very aware of their need to eat and drink. However, as time passes, moms are motivated to get their pre-

pregnancy body back and tend to skimp on calories as breast feeding continues. The inadequate intake of food and fluids can lead to diminished milk supply and unsatisfying feeds. When this happens, babies tend to be fussy at the breast since "the restaurant" is not serving all the baby needs. This can also cause the baby to nurse more frequently and wake more during the night, causing more stress to both the babies and the parents.

When it comes to sleep, milk intake is most parents' main concern. Having tools for increasing milk supply is key. I highly recommend relief bottles: bottles (usually of breast milk) that can be given by a partner, nanny, or caregiver instead of Mom. It is imperative that one relief bottle be started early in the baby's life (between weeks two and four) so the baby learns to eat from a bottle as well as the breast. This allows the breast-feeding mother some flexibility to be away from the baby and an opportunity to get some rest. One relief bottle a day can be incorporated into the baby's feeding schedules. This is especially important for moms returning to work.

The American Academy of Pediatrics encourages breast feeding for one full year. While this may not be for every family, having the tools for successful breast feeding will help each family make the decision that is right for them and their babies.

If you are struggling with supply and getting discouraged by soreness, but don't feel that you need a lactation consultant quite yet, you can try the following home remedies to help keep your milk flowing:

Carolyn's "Sore Nipples No More" Recipe
For poor nipples that are cracked and swollen:

1. Fill a coffee mug with water.
2. Put two black tea bags in the water.
3. Heat the mug for 1 minute in the microwave.
4. Let the teabags cool off a bit, and place one on each nipple for twenty-five minutes.

Be careful not to let any water from the tea bags leak onto your clothing or that white sofa that you bought before having children. Tea bag residue will leave a permanent, not-so-timeless brown stain. For easy and instant relief, place refrigerated cabbage leaves on your nipples each time after nursing.

Carolyn's Supply-Boosting Float Recipe
1. Put two heaping spoonsful of vanilla ice cream in a tall glass.
2. Pour Guinness Stout on top of the ice cream.
3. Enjoy!

This delicious concoction includes these benefits:

- Hops, a grain known to relax you.
- Barley, a grain with eight amino acids that provide nutrients.
- Calcium, to ensure you keep your levels up so you don't suffer bone loss.
- Alcohol. Who doesn't need a little of that once in a while?

It's best to drink a Guinness float after your final feeding of the day, or when you're not going to breast-feed for at least two hours.

Formula Is Not a Four-Letter Word

A lot of times we work with clients who are struggling with breast feeding and would love to wean. However, they have objections to switching their babies to formula. Maybe they feel it's not fair to give their baby formula, or maybe they want to keep breast feeding because their baby nurses herself to sleep and they're terrified of taking away the one thing that works.

By no means do we want to suggest that breast feeding isn't the best option, but for some mothers, there's a cost to producing breast milk. Having to pump more than three times a day is pretty overwhelming and doesn't leave much time for other things, like getting outside or taking a desperately needed nap. If breast feeding exclusively means you have to be tethered to a breast pump all day for months on end, you might ask yourself if this feels like the best choice for your family.

If you have to supplement or switch to formula entirely, don't feel defeated. Your first job as a parent is to feed the baby. If you don't have enough breast milk, formula is a wonderful option. Pro-breast-feeding movements are well intentioned, but with so much attention on the benefits of breast feeding, we often find that some mothers feel inadequate over their personal supply situation and become unnecessarily depressed because they decided to add a little formula to their routine.

If you decide to make the switch and are having trouble getting your baby to accept the new flavor of formula, here's a way to ease the transition:

Days 1 and 2	Mix 25 percent formula with 75 percent breast milk for all bottles.
Days 3 and 4	Mix 50 percent formula with 50 percent breast milk for all bottles.
Days 4 and 5	Mix 75 percent formula with 25 percent breast milk for all the bottles.
Day 6	You're now on 100 percent formula.

Even if you aren't introducing formula, it's still a good idea to get your child used to taking breast milk from a bottle. According to Carolyn Migliore, Dream Team Baby's breast-feeding expert, it's best to wait to introduce a bottle until two weeks of age. If you give a baby a bottle once a week (some encourage once a day) after that point, it'll make her flexible and won't cause nipple confusion. This way, if anything ever renders you unable to breast-feed (for example,

Conner had a lengthy hospital stay when her son was three months old), you'll be reassured she'll be able to eat without difficulty.

Babies Six to Twelve Months Old: Introducing Solids

If you thought your baby was messy before, this is the time they are really going to show you what they are made of. Head to the store and buy detergent in bulk. You'll need it for the months ahead.

Between six and twelve months, most of your baby's fat and calories should still come predominantly from breast milk or formula. Most babies still have between three to five milk feedings per day; however, as they go from six months of age to one year, their total daily milk intake will drop—starting out around twenty-eight to thirty-two ounces daily and reducing to approximately twenty to twenty-four ounces by one year of age.

Developmentally it makes sense to add solids at this time: your baby is now on the move and needs extra sustenance to push herself up and begin cruising around. Her movements are now much more deliberate. By six months, children are grabbing (beware of your dangling earrings) and putting all kinds of objects in their mouths.

Feeding time offers great practice for these new milestones. On top of developing your baby's hand-eye coordination and adding some substance to your baby's feedings, consuming solids also helps with language development. It takes a lot of jaw and tongue control to chew foods, and your baby will appreciate being vocally in shape when it's time to say, "Mommy!"

Unless your pediatrician has directed you to do otherwise, always use breast milk or formula to make cereal, not water. Most babies need extra calories wherever they can get them.

There are many schools of thinking on how to start solids, and no definitive right or wrong way to do it. Often, adding solids is culturally based and largely reflective of your own history and relationship with food. There are many ways to introduce solids, but this section contains advice that's been successful for our clients. Of course, if your pediatrician has advised you to add solids differently, you should follow his or her advice.

We like starting with oatmeal as a first solid because it's less constipating than rice cereal; still, a lot of people choose to start with rice cereal because it can be easier to digest. Once your baby's body has shown it can properly eat and digest basic grains, it's time to experiment with pureed foods. You'll know your baby is ready when she has figured out how to swallow grains (taking it from a spoon and no longer pushing all of it completely out of her mouth) and you've waited a few days to ensure no negative reaction.

We like to think of our babies' meals as breakfast, lunch, and dinner and serve our babies food we'd traditionally eat at those meals. For instance, keep oatmeal as your baby's breakfast and add a fruit. Next, add a yellow vegetable for lunch and dinner to your baby's cereal, and then a green vegetable at lunch and dinner. Over the next months, you'll continue adding new vegetables, as well as other proteins, grains, and fruits. We recommend that parents offer a variety of pureed foods to their babies for each meal, because babies are similar to us: they like variety, they prefer certain foods over others, and they get bored of certain flavors too.

Your meals will look like this:

Breakfast	Oatmeal or rice cereal and fruit.
Lunch	One green vegetable (green beans, peas, spinach), one yellow vegetable (sweet potatoes, carrots, squash), protein (chicken, beef, tofu, lentil), and fruit for dessert.
Dinner	One green vegetable (green beans, peas, spinach), one yellow vegetable (sweet potatoes, carrots, squash), protein (chicken, beef, tofu, lentil), and fruit for dessert.

Remember how uncomfortably constipated you could get during your pregnancy? The same thing can happen to your baby's digestive system starting between four and six months, often coinciding when he starts solids. If you notice your child's elimination schedule hits the skids (pun intended), try adding some pureed prunes each morning with his regular oatmeal. This magic elixir will get things moving and make for a happier baby. Beware! Prunes are a breakfast food only. If you offer them later in the day, their explosive nature can have a negative impact on your baby's sweet dreams.

Once you start adding solids, it's best to add new foods about three days apart so you know which food is the culprit if your child has a negative reaction. For instance, some babies are allergic to milk, eggs, soy, wheat, or peanuts, and you'll generally know if your baby is in this group if you notice a rash, diarrhea, or vomiting within a few hours of serving a new food. Some food allergies are more serious than others. If your baby has a swollen mouth or is having difficulty breathing after eating something new, call 911 and your pediatrician immediately.

Sometimes your baby can have a food intolerance or difficulty digesting a particular food versus an all-out allergic reaction. Symptoms like diarrhea, bloating, or gas will be more evident with intolerance, but these reactions could resolve themselves as your baby grows. That's why it's always a good idea to keep a food diary—or you can talk to your pediatrician about when it might be best to try a questionable food again.

Around seven months, start adding thicker textures of foods; between eight and nine months, your baby's going to start experimenting with table foods, like small pieces of easily chewed food you're eating. Adding really overcooked orzo to veggies is a great start.

By eight to nine months, try to place finger foods on your baby's tray so he can start practicing feeding himself. We love to put peas and round oat cereal on the tray; they're easy to pick up and they're sweet, so your baby will enjoy participating in the feast.

Between nine and eleven months, your baby will start to eat toddler versions of foods you eat. You'll still be feeding her some pureed veggies, but the main meal should be soft table foods that require more chewing action—for example, pasta mixed with bits of chicken or ham, tiny bits of pancake, baked potato, or broiled fish. By your child's first birthday, she should be able to stuff a huge cupcake in her mouth, an American rite of passage. By twelve months, she'll also be able to chew overly cooked green beans, squash, sweet potatoes, peas—really, any table food—so you should feel comfortable ditching the baby food around this time.

Here are some tips for getting your child to eat more during meals:

+ *Use common sense when feeding your baby.* Just as you get bored of flavors, your baby gets bored too, so offer several flavors throughout the meal. Put everything you are going to serve your baby on one plate, and let him sample it all. It doesn't matter that he eats everything; when he's done, he's done.

+ *When your baby is about nine months, do a flavor check.* Try not to overwhelm your child with sophisticated flavors, but if the food you're giving your baby doesn't taste good to you, it's possible your child won't like it either. It's totally okay to start roasting sweet potatoes in olive oil or adding butter to steamed green beans to make them more appealing.

+ *Offer the pure flavors of the food you serve so your child will develop a taste for them.* If you always mix pureed peas with pureed squash, your child may not like peas or squash on its own when it's time to eat steamed peas or broiled squash.

+ *Always give your child a spoon or fork to hold.* This will encourage her tactile abilities.

+ *Share a meal with your child.* Your baby has watched you and your spouse share food. Try to feed your baby where solids are eaten: at the table. Also, if you're eating while your baby eats, you're less likely to hover, which will give your child the chance to practice on his own a bit.

"If you need more motivation to share meal time with your kids, research shows that children in families who share meals are more likely to eat healthier as they grow up and are less likely to suffer from obesity or diabetes. If that's not enough, researchers have also found fewer instances of teenage pregnancy, drug abuse, and depression in children whose families have meals together."

—DR. AMY DEMATTIA, PEDIATRICIAN

Don't forget water! Try to offer a little water with each meal. At first, your baby may not understand how to drink from a cup, but after three meals a day, every day, she'll soon be reaching for the cup herself. This will help in weaning from the bottle and the breast around the time she's twelve months.

Babies Twelve to Eighteen Months Old: Ditching Bottles and Switching to Whole Milk and More Solids

At this point, there are some key changes that signal your baby is graduating to toddlerhood. Temper tantrums are one, and walking and climbing another, and both require a lot of energy. Babies of this age are ready to drink whole milk, and liquids are taking more of a back seat to solids.

We're assuming your baby is not allergic to cow's milk. If your baby has a milk allergy, consult with your pediatrician to see what kind of milk is best.

When your baby is ready to switch to whole milk, we recommend trying the same technique we suggest when adding formula:

Days 1 and 2	Mix 25 percent whole milk with 75 percent breast milk or formula for all bottles.
Days 3 and 4	Mix 50 percent whole milk with 50 percent breast milk or formula for all bottles.
Days 4 and 5	Mix 75 percent whole milk with 25 percent breast milk or formula for all bottles.
Day 6	You're now on 100 percent whole milk.

Transition from Bottle to Sippy Cup

Once your baby is drinking only cow's milk, it's time to graduate from the bottle to a sippy cup. It can be hard to make the switch completely, especially if you notice your child consumes considerably less from a sippy cup than she did when drinking from a bottle. However, try to avoid leaving one bottle in the routine, because it can interfere with your baby's incentive to take milk from another source.

Many speech and language specialists recommend sippy cups over bottles at twelve months. They help prepare the mouth for language development and acquisition.

The best time to try switching to sippy cups is in the morning, because this is when your baby is the hungriest. You may get her to take only three ounces the first time. But if you keep offering sippy cups at the same time you offer bottles or breast-feed, your baby will catch on within forty-eight hours or so. Make sure that you offer lots of good food during mealtimes, so you know your baby isn't missing out on nourishment.

If your child is around twenty-four months and still very attached to the bottle, you may want to consider having a farewell gathering party. Look through all your diaper bags, cabinets, and anywhere else a bottle might be. Have your baby help you put all the bottles in a bag and then explain that the Bottle Fairy is coming that night to get the bottles. Now that he's big enough to use sippy cups, it's time for new babies to have his old bottles. Replace the bag with a toy as a gift from the fairy for your child to discover in the morning. This can work with some children, but the best bet is to phase out bottles around twelve months and avoid such an elaborate good-bye.

Experimentation and Independence

Other than needing to cut up fruit, vegetables, and protein so your child won't choke, your baby should be eating the same table food as you do most of the time. Take your baby with you to dim sum and don't bring grilled cheese as a backup—and when you make your famous roasted chicken, don't offer a mac and cheese option. The more variety you add and the closer your baby's food looks to what you are eating, the more open your child will be to different foods.

This is also the time to ensure your baby has a spoon and fork with each meal. While you may still have to spoon soup and other more pureed foods for your baby, try to let your baby feed herself as much as possible. Making sure you're hungry at the same time your baby is will help you focus on your own food more and help you hold back a bit, so your baby will have the opportunity to learn. Your challenge is to have your baby eating mostly on her own by eighteen months.

Sweet Dreams!

It's important to keep in mind the respective benefits of both breast and bottle feeding when you plan to introduce solid foods into your baby's diet. In fact, your baby's eating habits are a huge factor in her ability to learn how to sleep peacefully throughout the night. Once you are following a feeding schedule, all you need to do is build a strong support team and figure out how to keep your emotions in check as you approach sleep teaching.

One Dad's Perspective: Pregnancy, Birth, and Sleep

DAVID B., DAD TO LUCY

When we learned that my wife was pregnant, the first thing I thought was how fortunate we were because it happened so quickly for us. We have many friends for whom it took months and even years to make it past the dreaded first trimester and into the safe-to-tell-family-and-friends zone. The second thought I had once I learned my wife was pregnant was, "Am I really ready for this?" I started asking all the dads I knew if they had been ready. The answer was unanimous: a man is never ready for a baby. But the fear of the upcoming birth was tempered once we entered the calm eye of the pregnancy, otherwise known as the second trimester. The nausea had subsided, and my wife was again comfortable.

Enter the third trimester.

Nothing prepares you for the weeks leading up to the birth of your first child. Clothes don't fit your wife, and she feels huge. She can't sleep through the night. And you'd better do what she says, because with all those hormones going off, she may just kill you. Think about it: she is so big that no sleeping position allows her to nap very long. If she even looks at water, she has to pee. The poor woman doesn't have the luxury of a glass or two of wine to take the edge off. And if she gets sick—well, she has to suck it up because she is not allowed to have medicine. Could I carry a baby to term? I honestly don't think so.

As the projected delivery date closed in, I found myself feeling that my life would never be the same—or perhaps it was because all my friends kept telling me that. What kind of father would I be?

Lucy was born on June 22, 2010. Words cannot describe how proud I was to be a part of that moment. I held my wife's hand through the birth and the subsequent stitches. She was much stronger than I could ever be. She is amazing.

The weeks after the birth were exhausting for my wife. Lucy was feeding all hours of the day and night. The only person she was interested in was Mom. During this time, I felt like I was unable to contribute. What was I good for?

Soon enough, Lucy started gaining weight, and she was able to sleep longer between feeds at night. At this point, my wife and I decided we needed to try to put her on a schedule, but we were unsure where to begin. There were so many conflicting resources out there, and it was quite overwhelming. However, a few things were clear: Mommy needed more sleep, Daddy needed to become more involved, and our baby was crying out for structure (though we didn't know that's what she meant). Then we found Dream Team Baby.

I had no idea what to expect when our Dream Team Baby sleep consultant came to our home that first evening. Could Lucy really go to bed at 8:00 P.M. after months of going to bed at all hours of the night? She cried for a while. It was difficult to listen to at first. Finally a little after 8:30 P.M., Lucy surrendered to the inevitable sleep that lay before her. She was asleep well before our 9:00 P.M. TV shows had even started. Whoa!

The approach that Dream Team Baby used with our family did more than give my daughter a daily schedule to live by. It allowed a sense of normalcy to return to our lives. Now that I was armed with the knowledge, I was able to help my wife keep our daughter on track. In fact, Lucy's schedule was so easy to follow that my wife and I were able to sneak out for our first dinner together since the birth. I was on my way to getting my wife back!

In the first few weeks of implementing this new schedule, my wife really needed me to help her resist the temptation to run to Lucy's rescue when she was crying after putting her down at night. In those tense moments, I would go through my Dream Team Baby checklist: Baby had lovey, a fresh diaper, the perfect sleeping environment, and the necessary amount of milk to carry her through the night. And guess what? It worked every time. My new role helped my wife have confidence in me and allowed her to relax. Before I knew it, I had transformed from the guy who was scared about being a new dad to a father who had found his groove.

CHAPTER 7

Setting Up a Support System

W e've stopped counting the number of moms who ask us to help them teach their babies to sleep when their partners are out of town. Our answer is *always no*. It's not that we don't understand why they think this is an easier solution; it's simply that a partner must be involved and, at the very least, completely supportive. Having both parents (or the custodial one if it's a single-parent household) actively participate is vital to developing your child's healthy, secure habits in the long term.

Keys to Zzs

- **Synchronize as early as possible.** Both parents should agree on the plan to sleep-teach.
- **Declare independence from sleepless nights.** This will help you both keep strong when the going gets tough—and help you to nurture each other when you most need it.
- **Communicate your needs with one another.** Knowing exactly what your partner needs to feel nurtured makes it easier for you

to take care of each other. Healthy adult relationships are necessary to nourish healthy, sleeping babies.

- **Establish an effective support network.** Choose positive, encouraging people you can rely on in times of need or just for a break.

~~~~~~

We can't predict how your child is going to respond during sleep teaching. Truthfully, almost all children hit a bump in the road once in a while. So even if you or your partner takes a backseat on the initial sleep teaching, chances are you'll both be around for some difficult moments that surely lie ahead. If you "fix" sleep when your partner is out of town for work, he's going to come home and be confused as to why you're responding in certain ways to your child. His questioning may even be enough to throw you off course and go back to the old way to interacting with your child at night. We strongly encourage both parents to participate and learn at the same time. This way, you can both be equally effective in taking care of your baby, and your baby will never feel confused by getting mixed messages from you.

Most important, it's lonely at 3:00 A.M. when your baby is struggling to fall back asleep. You will want—and need—support from your partner. The middle of the night is when it's the easiest to give up if you don't have a partner who's on board and understands the benefits of the process. We completely agree and commiserate with one of our clients who said, there's nothing worse than that "whisper fighting" that goes on in the middle of the night when parents aren't aligned.

Ideally, start sleep teaching on a night when both parents are at home for bedtime. That way, you'll have each other for support and show a united and loving front to your child.

You should seriously question your partner when he or she says, "I don't care what we do to get the baby to sleep." Although a declaration like that may come from a good place, it's rarely true. Helping your child change requires both of you to change. It's work for everyone—more in the short term, but still some in the long term.

Good sleeping habits can easily unravel if you stop paying attention to your actions. That means both partners need to fully understand and commit to the process they're using.

Compose a Declaration of Independence

Before you begin sleep teaching, sit down with your partner one night after dinner and write out a "declaration of independence" from sleepless nights. Create a list of all the reasons you are sleep teaching. We created a contract for sleep teaching (see Appendix C) to help you and your partner stay motivated and committed when your minds start pouring out excuses to stop sleep teaching. If you're tempted to throw in the towel, pull out your list or contract to help you regain your strength.

We'll help you get started. Here are a few common reasons you may want to sleep-teach:

"Better sleep is what's best for my baby."

"We'll all have more balance in our lives, and that will make us all happier."

"I'm so exhausted that I'm having a hard time enjoying these precious moments with my baby."

"I'll be a better parent to my child—happier and more engaged—and that will help her self-esteem."

"Our baby is old enough to be an independent sleeper."

Healthy Relationships: Key to Bonding with Babies

by Dr. Ingrid Schweiger, psychotherapist

No one likes to hear a baby cry. Crying raises our anxiety and immediately makes us think, "What's wrong?" Very quickly, though, we begin to ask ourselves as new parents, "What am *I* doing wrong?"

Sleep training forces us to confront this anxiety. We ask ourselves over and over again, "If my baby is crying, am I a bad parent who is potentially doing something to hurt my child?" When our baby cries, we want to help her feel better not only for her sake but also to feel better about ourselves as parents.

I have worked with many couples suffering from severe sleep deprivation resulting from their fears about sleep training and their unwillingness to allow their babies to cry. The conflicts that arise for parents due to a lack of sleep in these situations are overwhelming, often interfering significantly in the bonding between parent and baby. Couples fight over how to respond, or not, to a baby's crying.

Parents who are exhausted and fighting communicate their conflict and anxiety to their baby. Even couples who commit to a formal sleep training program find it challenging to maintain a united front if and when the crying escalates.

I believe that parents need their sleep as much as the baby needs his sleep. Bonding requires emotional and physical energy. If a substantial portion of your physical and emotional energy is depleted due to exhaustion and conflict with your partner, there is not enough energy to bond with your baby.

Sleep deprivation also leads to depression, and depressed parents are less responsive to their babies. This is especially true when parents are always in conflict with each other. Parents who are rested are not only emotionally available to bond with their baby but also emotionally available to bond with each other as new parents. The greatest gift a couple can give to their baby is a happy and strong parental relationship, and that requires sleep. A healthy relationship nourishes your baby's development.

The transition to parenthood is not easy. Reaching out for professional support during and after pregnancy to work out any of the difficulties in your relationship can be helpful. If you and your partner are in conflict often about how to sleep-teach your baby, seek the help of a professional to discuss your thoughts, fears, and anxieties. You need to be united in order to have the physical and emotional energy for bonding with your baby and for making your transition to a healthy parenthood.

Even the most motivated and determined parents are susceptible to thoughts of defeat and despair. To make you feel understood, we've listed some common feelings you will most likely have until the moment your baby is a successful sleeper. We'll discuss each of these in more detail in Part Three of this book, but we wanted to mention them here so you aren't surprised when they pop into your head later. Also, just setting them down in writing takes some of the power out of these thoughts:

"My baby's going to hate his room."

"My baby's going to hate me."

"Crying is going to make my baby sick."

"She's going to have bad dreams about this that are going to haunt her for the rest of her life."

"I'm a terrible parent because I'm right here and I could easily make his crying stop."

"My job is to protect, and now I'm teaching my child that I won't be there for her."

"My baby and I are going to lose our close relationship, because he isn't sleeping with me anymore, which means he's going to turn to pornography and drugs later in life."

"This is how serial killers are created." A client's nanny actually said this to the mom—right before they found a new nanny.

These fears stem from an insecurity that comes from the unknown. Parents who have successfully taught their child to sleep know that none of these concerns actually comes to fruition, but you can't help having these thoughts anyway. So have someone to turn to for support and love throughout this process to make sure you can make it through.

> *"Sleep teaching will work, but it needs, time, patience, and a support system. There were many nights I had to walk out of the house and let my husband take over. And that is okay. You have to really partner with each other. We still toast our wine glasses about it all the time a year later!"*
> —KIM J., MOM TO LUCAS

Another unhappy side effect of letting these fears take over is that they can distract you from your baby's successes. Since your child is the one who has to do all the learning, though, the attention should go to her first. You can easily talk yourself out of anything, but that's only your mind playing tricks on you to get you to do what is easiest for you in the moment—which is to stop sleep teaching. When you can begin to put your child's needs above your own insecurities, sleep falls into place, and peace and tranquility become the new normal.

> *"As a new parent, one doesn't realize what children are capable of doing; in terms of sleeping, this is the only area where we accept mediocre development throughout the years, and there's no reason why we should."*
> —YADIRA D., MOM TO JOSIAH

If your partner is not supportive but you are desperate to help your baby sleep better, find a relative or friend who has already successfully used the method you've chosen—someone who will be there for you to call if you need help. Having someone you can call who loves you unconditionally is very helpful. But we also recommend you keep an emotional door open so there is a place in your heart to let your partner back in when he or she realizes what a chump he or she was for leaving you to do all the hard work on your own.

The Nurture Exercise

Parents need sleep just as much as children do. It's hard to be a supportive, attentive parent (and partner) if you're drained and feeling overly extended. To make sure you and your partner are a team and that you both have the energy to be strong for each other and your baby, we ask parents to do an exercise our in-house psychotherapist, Dr. Ingrid Schweiger, created. We call it the nurture exercise. It's a way for parents to communicate with each other about the things that make them feel cared for, happy, and loved.

> Even if you and your partner feel as if you take good care of each other, you could be working from an outdated playlist. The things that used to make you feel happy and satisfied before you had children may not necessarily be the things you treasure today. Maybe you used to love a date after work at a wine bar, but now what you really need is a half-hour alone with a gossip magazine.

Just so you can get an idea of what we mean, here are the nurture lists from a family we worked with:

Mom's Nurture List
1. A full night of uninterrupted sleep
2. Being held by my husband during happy times, not-so-happy times, and for no reason at all
3. A back massage by my husband

4. A massage or facial at a spa
5. Exercise followed by a long, hot shower that I can enjoy because I know that my baby is in good, capable hands
6. Spending a day in the park with just my husband and baby featuring a picnic, Scrabble, and long walks
7. Dinner alone with my husband with delicious food and my favorite wine
8. Seeing my parents, siblings, and nieces and nephew play with and go crazy over my son and how elated he is by the attention
9. Chocolate
10. Fresh homemade chocolate chip cookies
11. A brief weekend with just my husband
12. Taking a nap in the sun on a warm day
13. Being completely and totally organized

Dad's Nurture List
1. Driving fast with the roof down and the radio blasting—alone (even if it's just in my imagination)
2. Eating a blueberry pie (for breakfast)
3. Taking a nap on the couch
4. Watching a ball game while eating a thin-crust pizza with ham, pineapple, and olives
5. Not shaving
6. Anything to do with chocolate
7. Watching movies that will never be nominated for an Oscar
8. A visit to a favorite place
9. New T-shirts
10. A clean, uncluttered, apartment
11. Over-ordering

It may have been a long time since you thought about yourself and your needs. That's exactly why this exercise is so important. Airplane safety messages say, "Put on your air mask first [in case of an emergency] and then help your child." In the same way, sleep teaching takes focus and attention, and it's hard to be strong, emotionally present, and encouraging if you are gasping for air. So take a few minutes and try to come up with a few things that nurture you.

Here are the rules:

- *Find a quiet space alone, and make a list of all the things that make you feel nurtured.* They can be things your partner does and things you need in your life. Keep in mind that the more options you put on your list, the easier it'll be for your partner to take care of you. But put too many things on the list, and your partner may not be aware of the more important items. We think that about five to ten items is best.

- *Share your list with your partner, and try not to be offended if something you do out of love is not on the list.* It just means if you want to really nurture your partner, you can focus your energy on other things.

- *Do one thing on your partner's list each day, particularly during sleep teaching.* In fact, it's a great thing to keep up forever. If you're a single parent, make the list for yourself. Post it where you can see it, and do something for yourself each day during teaching.

- *If your partner doesn't do something on your list one day, don't mention it.* Instead, channel that annoyance by focusing on your partner's list instead. A partner who is so stressed that he or she forgot to nurture you may be having a hard time and need more attention from you. The more you take care of your partner, the more energy he or she will have to help take care of you.

- *If your partner's feeling a little awkward but tries to do something on your list anyway and it's a huge bomb, don't mention it.* Share only comments of gratitude. The easiest way to get someone to never do something again is to criticize him or her. Very rarely do things happen perfectly the first time. Try to remember that the attempt to take care of you is a sign of love.

Just because you aren't actively involved in something on your partner's list (for example, you aren't tagging along to "play golf with the guys") doesn't mean you're off the hook for those particular nurture items. Pay attention to the last time your wife got a facial or the last time your husband spent time with his friends and help them make time to do those things. By ensuring your partner's sense of well-being, this will make him or her happier and more energetic when it's time to be a strong parent.

Sweet Dreams!

Happier partners = happier relationship = happier children.

Worrisome thoughts can easily derail your greatest efforts, even if you have done everything else we've suggested in preparation for sleep teaching. You owe it to your baby to have the support you need lined up in advance, so you can stay strong and confident throughout the sleep teaching process.

CHAPTER 8

Keeping Emotional Issues in Check

By this point, you've done a lot—and it's all going to pay off soon.

The last piece on preparing for sleep teaching is getting your head in the game. We suggest you read this chapter even if you're not planning to dive into Part Three of this book right now. The previous chapters have given you a different way of thinking about sleep, plus some tools to help your child sleep better. We hope you are ready to put the wheels into motion. However, if you're not doing that yet, this chapter might encourage you to keep working for an even better sleeping situation.

Keys to Zzzs

- **Be prepared for challenges.** Accept the possibility, and the likelihood, of struggle along the way to better sleep.
- **Put your frustration in perspective.** Things are usually not as intense as they seem.
- **Combat your fear of sleep training.** You can do this!

- **Examine your feelings about crying.** Try to separate your own feelings from your baby's crying in healthy ways.
- **Reason out negative feelings.** They only create guilt and result in setbacks.

~~~~~~

Before you start our sleep teaching plan—or any other sleep teaching method—it's important to remember that your child will likely struggle at some point in the process. Babies are understandably frustrated as they learn to sleep in an entirely new way. Remember that frustration with change is normal and is actually a key part of the human learning process.

No one likes frustration, but we can learn to appreciate it. Frustration pushes us to problem-solve and leads us to new understandings, from the negative, "Arrrghh! This change stinks!" to the more positive, "What can I do to make this situation better?"

Reminding yourself that you're allowed to be uncomfortable part of the time is a good idea, because it's going to help you to remain more patient when your child becomes frustrated during sleep teaching—or, really, at any other time.

You Don't Have to Be Afraid

There are countless reasons we encourage you to wait before starting sleep teaching with your child. Feeling afraid of what may happen isn't one of those reasons. If your approach to sleep teaching is well rounded (and we believe ours is) and you're consistent, you'll start to see progress quickly—for some, almost immediately.

If you want to understand how much of an impact proper instruction has, imagine a lovely spring day in your neighborhood. You see your neighbor in his driveway with his daughter, Tess. He's introducing her to a new training-wheel-free bike. As you watch this special rite of passage, you notice that Tess is very wobbly and a little nervous at the start of her first lesson. But her dad keeps encouraging her and praising every small bit of progress she makes. Although Tess is far from mastering bike riding the first day, her dad is very proud of her efforts. He gives her a huge hug of congratulations when the lesson is over.

The next day they're at it again. Tess is still struggling, but she's getting a little steadier, and Dad is cheering her on every step of the way. By the next week, Tess is almost ready to join the professional BMX team. She is much more confident and owns her new skill, going over bumps and turning circles. She has learned how to do it all by herself and is very proud.

Now imagine a different version of that same scenario. This time as Tess's dad wheels out her new bike, he looks reluctant and somewhat unsure about how this lesson is going to go down. In fact, he tells her he's not sure she's ready, that she might fall, but they're going to "give it a try, I guess." While Tess struggles to balance and pedal without her training wheels, her dad cringes every time she struggles. Whenever she starts to wobble, he rushes over, grabs the handlebars, stops her, and gives her a worried hug of reassurance. When she doesn't master riding her bike the first day, her dad decides she's not ready and puts things on hold for a few months.

This is an absolutely understandable situation; we've all probably done this to our children in some form. But knowing that Tess could have had a positive experience instead of a negative one is disappointing, to say the least.

Riding a bike and learning to be an independent sleeper are the same in that both are learned skills that take practice and patience. Most parents would never expect their children to master riding a bike the first day. Yet we see many parents who do expect their children to learn independent sleeping within a day or two. Although many parents will see dramatic results in the first few days, it sometimes takes several weeks, or even months, for children to become true masters of this new skill.

When you decided to have a child, you signed an invisible yet rock-solid contract to become your baby's biggest fan. Have you ever seen cheerleaders lose their cool when the team is down? No: they wear their faith as a badge of honor. And if you practice having that same faith in your child, there is no limit to what she can achieve. Steadfast and unwavering strength is within you, but it's also a skill that needs to be cultivated. We realize this is not always easy. But remember that giving your baby a chance to show you he can do it without you will start a new kind of relationship based on support and mutual respect.

Listen to how these parents met the sleep teaching challenge:

"I thought every time my son cried at night, he needed me or something from me. You really opened my eyes to the fact that there comes a time when babies really just need to learn to put themselves back to sleep, and that can be frustrating for them. Knowing this made it easier for me to hear him cry, because I knew that by not running into the room, I was giving him the space and independence he needed to figure out how to get back to sleep. This changed everything for us, and within two nights, he was suddenly sleeping twelve hours and not crying out during the night. This also made me think about the bigger picture of parenting: you can't always run in and rescue a child from a moment of frustration. I've learned to take a step back and give him a chance to work through things on his own."

—DANIELLE M., MOM TO JOSEPH

"I remember feeling so anxious and panicked the day you were scheduled to arrive. Even though you were great about assuring us that Joshie was not going to just 'cry,' I knew there would be some crying, and it broke my heart. Once we got Joshie down for the night, you kept saying, 'You know Joshie can do this! You know he can! Tell him how proud you are of him!' That kept me going. Joshie now sleeps like a champ, and we are so, so thankful."

—NEIL AND GALIT E., PARENTS OF JOSHUA

What About Crying?

We haven't even gotten to the part of the book where we tell you how to get your baby from needing you to fall asleep to being able to sleep beautifully on her own, but we're guessing you've figured out that it will likely involve some amount of crying. It's true that our method of teaching children to love sleep does usually involve some initial frustration.

When young children are frustrated, they cry. Crying doesn't always mean children are afraid, hurting, hungry, lonely, or mad at you. It can also mean your baby is frustrated, confused, annoyed, tired, slightly uncomfortable, or just blowing off steam. The key is to identify these types of cries in your child. We'll help you figure out how to do that like the expert you are in your child's life.

Hearing your baby cry and holding back for a moment to allow him the chance to fix the situation himself is not being a bad parent; it's being a thoughtful one. We know you've heard your baby cry because he was hungry, and we imagine you fed him then. But babies also cry because they are tired, and helping your child get sleep when he is tired is also your job. Similarly, if you work to help your child form healthy eating habits, even though breast feeding is a struggle to begin with or taking a bottle isn't what your baby wants to do despite your lack of milk supply, teaching your child to be an independent sleeper can work the same way. It's a handful of tough days, followed by periods of bliss.

If you're worried about what allowing your baby to cry says about you as a parent, try to think about teaching your baby to sleep as if it was just as important for her well-being as being buckled into a car seat. If your child protests while being placed into a car seat, she'll likely cry. But do you feel that you are a bad parent for ignoring her frustrated cries? Would you instead decide, "My child knows best, so I'll follow her lead and let her ride on my lap for this trip?" Certainly not!

You'd simply drive to the grocery store, listening to your baby fuss and cry in her car seat—even if it lasts for the entire trip. When you arrive at the store, you might take a deep breath and high-five yourself for making it through the drive—because you did what you had to do to keep your baby safe. You get your baby out of the car seat and move on. You wouldn't walk through the grocery store replaying the scene in your mind over and over, wondering if you've caused irreparable damage to your child by "making her" cry. Yet that's exactly what so many parents do to themselves unnecessarily when their baby cries at night.

"If your baby is tired and crying and you've solved all the other problems—he's not hungry, he's not sick, his diaper is clean, and he is safe in his crib—then the solution is sleep. These cries are your baby's way to communicate that he needs sleep."

—DR. AMY DEMATTIA, PEDIATRICIAN

We encourage you to think about this car seat analogy whenever you feel that your baby needs you during the times you know she needs to be sleeping. Children don't always know best. You are the parent, so your job is to set the parameters and guide her to a healthy, loving, and supportive way of life. This is what helps your baby feel safe and secure, and it's good parenting. If you come away with any final thoughts after reading this book, we'd like you to focus on this one: caring enough to help your baby be healthy is an important way of showing your child love.

If you're starting to feel a little sad about the good possibility that you will have to let your baby cry, it could mean you aren't ready to start sleep teaching. Yes, you may be physically exhausted and think you want to sleep-teach, but if the thought of change makes

"Sleep education helped us persevere; knowing how important sleep is in the long run (not just the short-run, sleep-deprivation sense) and thinking of it as a crucial skill that Lucas had to learn like any other made it easier to handle the crying."

—NINA AND IRA, PARENTS OF LUCAS

"I asked my pediatrician for advice on my son's sleep issues, and he recommended Dream Team. He said how a child learns to sleep as a baby will affect the rest of his life, including his ability to perform in school and beyond. He said, 'You can't afford not to do this.' I was so motivated to complete the program successfully, knowing it was best for him to learn to sleep well."

—KIM J., MOM TO LUCAS

you want to cry because you're not ready for your new role and you're going to miss those intimate moments at night, then you may want to wait a little longer before you start to sleep-teach.

And if your baby is older than four months and you are feeling a little guilty because you think you waited too long to start working on sleep, we want to reassure you that you did the right thing. First, change is hard, especially when you have a newborn. Second, sometimes it's hard to see how capable our children really are. As parents, we can get frozen in time, and to us, that nine month old still looks like the newborn we fell in love with from his first breath. But if your child is over four months old and generally healthy, then he or she can learn to be an independent sleeper whenever you are ready to show him the way!

Ignore the Mompetition

Somewhere along the way we created sides: us versus them. On one side are the "anti-criers" and on the other are the "cry-it-out-ers." The truth is, we don't know many people who are solidly in either camp. There are times in parenting when we need to be emotionally there for our children. There are also times, sometimes on the same day, when we need to draw a line. So if that's the case, why do we have a need to alienate fellow parents who make different decisions than we would?

Being a parent is tough enough—and we all have to make the choices that make sense for our family. There's no "Most Loving Mom" or "Most Capable Dad" contest. We all know what's best for our families. Calling sleep teaching "cruel" or attachment parenting "unbalanced" is not productive or respectful. If something works for other parents, then great! Let's stop judging each other and start focusing energy on enjoying this precious time with our young children and doing what feels right for us.

Here's how one parent looks at it:

"If someone doesn't agree with what you're doing, then who cares? You're doing this for your family, not theirs. If sleep teaching is right for your family and it's working for you, don't listen to what anyone else is saying. I struggled a lot with sleep 'training' because I had told myself before I had my son that I wouldn't be doing cry methods or anything like that. Well, I realized that I had to let go of all those ideas because what I was doing wasn't working. It turned out that teaching my son to sleep was one of the best gifts I could give him and our family. It changed our lives. People really underestimate the power of sleep deprivation."
—HEATHER A., MOM TO WILLIAM

Sweet Dreams!

Remember not to feel too guilty about giving your child the space she needs in order to become a better sleeper. Parenting is all about giving and taking, helping and then stepping back. If your child is struggling with unhealthy sleeping patterns, it's time to take the unhealthy routine away and give her the environment to learn. She'll be so much better off in the long run, and you will be too. So take a deep breath and turn to the chapters in Part Three. You will be entering a whole new world.

A Full House and Twins Transformed

NOREEN C., MOM TO TOMMY, KIERAN, AND TWINS RILEY AND SEAN

At the time my twins were born, I had a son just about to turn three and a seventeen-month-old son, so the house was already in chaos.

The twins never slept. Sean had acid reflux, which complicated matters, and I think, now looking back, I was definitely suffering from either extreme exhaustion or postpartum depression. My husband works long hours on Wall Street, and the market was collapsing, so that was yet another stress. We were basically in turmoil. Then Dream Team Baby showed up, and in a few days we were able to regain control and for the first time really meet our twins.

What made us call for help? My family was falling apart. Everyone was suffering. I was getting so much advice, and it was overwhelming and confusing—and some was just wrong. I needed someone I could trust to tell me what to do. I was very skeptical at first, but I figured it was worth a try.

The advice I found most helpful was that everyone needs to be on board. As hard as it was to listen to the twins cry, it was just as hard to have my mom look at me with this look of, "What are you doing? These are your babies! Pick them up!" It really, really began to shake my confidence.

We had to sit my parents down and say, "This is what we are doing. We need you to respect it, even if you don't agree with it. It's making a hard situation harder when you look at me with doubt. I love these babies, and I know it may seem cruel, but these are experts in sleep, and I trust them. So if it's too hard for you to listen to the crying, then maybe you should stay away for a few days until we get settled. When all is said and done, you will need to follow the schedule and the program. Agreed?"

They *did* stay away, and they came back to what my mom still refers to as a miracle. The babies actually looked like different babies; they laughed and they were alert. I used to refer to them as little glass babies: if you even touched them, it would set them off. But not now. Now they're fun, and I realize this was the healthiest decision I made for them.

There was this moment when they were finally "awake" and came into their little personalities for what seemed like the first time ever. I remember saying, "Hi, Riley. Hi, Sean. I'm Mommy—a very well-rested mommy for the first time in a long time, just like you. It's nice to finally meet you."

I was kind of scared of having a schedule, but I quickly began to appreciate it. The best part was that I had these guaranteed breaks in the day, and I used every minute of them to give my older boys my full attention, and for that I was grateful. They were missing that, and it still makes me sad to think about it, but now I just say, "When the babies go down, we'll work on it."

PART THREE

Get Sleep!

Where the real work of sleep teaching
begins—and continues.

CHAPTER 9

Creating Your Lesson Plan

There's a reason teachers create lesson plans: it helps them be confident about their material, makes them more engaging instructors, and ensures they have time to cover the most important topics. And if by any chance they can't be in class, a lesson plan lets a substitute know exactly what to do.

Those are the same reasons we encourage you to be prepared when the day comes to teach your baby to sleep. The good news is that you've already done a lot of great groundwork if you've followed our advice in the first two parts of this book.

Now that you are ready for sleep teaching, here are the final steps for preparing your child to learn to sleep.

Keys to Zzzs

- **Gather your sleep supplies.** This list could include everything from black garbage bags and painter's tape to your child's lovey.
- **Pick a bedtime.** Sticking to a regular bedtime will help your child learn when it's time to sleep, so be as consistent as possible.

- **Choose a day to start.** If you have plans to travel or a huge meeting the next day, it might be best to wait until there's a better time to sleep-teach—without added stress.
- **Get your pediatrician's approval.** Your pediatrician may know about something (like a feeding challenge) that could have a negative effect on sleep teaching for your baby.
- **Give your child the sleeping space she needs.** Ideally, this should be as far away from people and distractions as possible.
- **Emotionally prepare toddlers for sleep teaching.** Getting toddlers ready before you start will help them ease into it more naturally.
- **Examine your daytime parenting.** How you parent during the day will have an enormous impact on what happens when it's bedtime.
- **Make sure your child will be safe at night.** Do a safety check around your child's nursery before sleep teaching so you won't worry as much about whether your baby's okay.
- **Involve siblings and caregivers.** Making sure everyone understands and agrees with the program is critical to success.

Go Shopping

In order to make sure you're prepared for anything that happens the first night of sleep teaching, here's a list of supplies to have on hand:

- Black garbage bags or temporary blackout paper shades
- Painter's tape (for protecting your window frames if you tape up garbage bags)
- White noise machine (with a continuous sound option)
- Room thermometer
- Your child's lovey

+ Footed pajamas
+ Extra crib sheets that are clean and accessible
+ For some, a crib tent

Crib Tent or No Crib Tent?

A crib tent is a domed mesh covering that attaches to the top of a crib, preventing toddlers from climbing out—and at Dream Team Baby, we have a love-hate relationship with them.

Crib tents can be good because they keep a baby safe in her crib. If you have a thirteen month old who likes to flop herself out of the crib using the sheer weight of her head, then a crib tent is an absolute gift. If your baby starts climbing out of a crib and you're not ready to sleep-teach, a crib tent is a great stop-gap measure. Once you're ready, you can remove the tent and teach your baby how to stay put at night.

But crib tents can also disguise a future problem: eventually you'll have to remove the tent, and then your child will be able to leave his room at night.

You can teach him to stay put much more easily when he has the four sides of a crib around him. When you do, stay close and put pillows and mattresses on the floor all around your child's crib (see the FAQs in Appendix A of this book).

Another upside of tackling crib climbing is that parents can trust their child to stay in a portable crib during a weekend at Grandma's!

Pick a Bedtime

Pick a bedtime that you can commit to in the relative long term. As a reminder, we recommend you choose a bedtime between 6:00 P.M. and 8:00 P.M. This is truly the best bedtime range for babies through children in grade school. It's also the point of the day when it's easiest for your child to fall asleep. Most parents choose 7:00 P.M. or 7:30 P.M.

If you're panicking because your family's schedule isn't going to permit having a bedtime between 6:00 P.M. and 8:00 P.M., try to think of it as a short-term commitment to start. Your primary goal is to make learning to sleep as easy as possible for your child. So for the first couple of weeks, you may have to make a few adjustments that are slightly inconvenient for you (for example, rearranging your own schedule to make sure you can put your baby to sleep by 8:00 P.M.). Once you see your baby sleeping so well, the solutions to certain obstacles or issues often reveal themselves. At worst, once your baby is sleeping well, you can make some modifications to his schedule to make it more sustainable for your family. If sleep falls apart when you change the schedule, you'll know that your baby is capable of sleeping through the night and you'll know what you changed, so you can get there again.

Pick a Day to Start

The day you begin sleep teaching is the day you commit to being totally consistent for your child for two weeks straight. That means consistency in how you respond to your baby, consistency in her naptimes and bedtimes, and consistency in where she sleeps. Two weeks probably seems like a long time now, but it's about how long most children need to master independent sleeping and get into the groove of their new lives.

Just because we say this is a two-week process doesn't mean you're going to have two weeks of intense nights. In fact, after the first few days, you'll probably be pinching yourself at how wonderful your new life is already. The two-week period we talk about is the time we want you to commit to consistency and putting your baby first when you make plans.

The first few days of sleep teaching may be exhausting. We normally suggest parents start sleep teaching on a Friday night. That's usually when most parents are home and don't have work the next day. You'll both be around for the naps (which can be a little hard at first), and you'll have an opportunity for some quality family time with your baby during the daytime.

Here are some common pitfalls that add a level of unnecessary stress to the sleep teaching process. Remember, the more stress you have, the harder it is for babies to learn. Is your start date:

+ *Too soon?* Make sure you have enough time to finish any necessary homework in this or previous chapters. Cutting corners means that you might not have time to fix something ahead of time that is preventing your baby from falling asleep. This is going to increase your baby's frustration, which means more crying.

+ *Coinciding with a major family transition?* If possible, choose a different date, especially if you know any of the following may be happening during the two weeks of sleep teaching. These take a parent's attention and energy away from the child, making it harder to stay consistent and focused:

  + Parent going back to work
  + Change in nanny or day care
  + Move to a new home
  + Arrival of a new baby
  + Older child starting school
  + Visit from a friend or relative

+ *Overlapping with a vacation or major celebration?* No matter where you make your baby's nursery, we encourage you to stay put for two weeks. If you own more than one residence or your baby is used to sleeping at Grandma's during the daytime, we would still consider sleep at these places as travel because your child has to sleep in a different room from the one in which he is accustomed to learning.

+ *Coinciding with a vaccination?* Sometimes immunizations can make a baby feel a little sore and run a low-grade fever. If you have to give immunizations before you begin, make sure you wait forty-eight hours after an immunization so you know if your child has any adverse reactions.

The goal is to take care of the things you can control so that any unforeseen circumstances aren't completely overwhelming and don't throw you off course.

If Possible, Get Your Pediatrician's Seal of Approval

Give yourself some peace of mind and confirm that your child is healthy before sleep teaching. If possible, schedule your child's regular well-baby appointment to take place a few days before you start sleep teaching. At this appointment, ask your doctor the following questions:

+ Is there anything that may physically prevent my child from learning how to sleep: an ear infection or a sore throat, for example?
+ Has my child's growth remained constant? As long as your baby's growth is sticking to a particular curve on a growth chart, growth shouldn't be an issue. If you are having trouble keeping your baby's weight consistent, then you should discuss the situation with your pediatrician to make sure it's advisable to remove any nighttime feedings.
+ Is it okay to begin sleep teaching?

If your well-baby visit is too far off and you are desperate to start sleep teaching, most pediatrician offices will allow you to come in for a quick exam for your baby. A nurse practitioner can give your little one a once-over and get your pediatrician's consent based on the results of the exam. If your doctor says your baby is healthy and medically capable of learning to sleep, it'll help you remain confident and consistent throughout sleep teaching.

Give Your Child the Sleeping Space She Needs

Children do best when they have a room of their own for sleep teaching. Here are some reasons that you should be motivated to ensure you baby has her own room for sleep teaching:

+ *If your baby can see you, she'll want you.* We can't stress this enough, especially if you're breast feeding. If you're sharing a room, we strongly urge you to sleep in another room during sleep teaching. Think about it this way. Your child has been a bit attached to you for sleep. You're now trying to break his nighttime dependency. When you're trying to give something up (like sweets), it's much harder to put it out of your mind if it's right there within reach. Don't tempt your child. Even if he can't physically see you in the space, he has an amazing sense of smell and will be able to sense your presence, particularly if you are breast feeding. This means you'll need to move out of your room temporarily. If your baby struggles a little more once you move back in, we recommend you get a screen or curtain to give your baby some privacy and eliminate distractions.

+ *Adults are loud sleepers.* Even if your baby isn't breast feeding, being in the same space during sleep teaching is ripe with potential land mines. We adults move, snore, cough, and even talk in our sleep. The last thing you want to do is accidently wake your baby up when she's done such hard work putting herself to sleep.

+ *Siblings don't always make the best of bedfellows.* If possible, don't ask your children to share a room until they're both sleeping through the night. Having a loud roommate who is up at all hours is annoying whether you're one or twenty-one years old. And one child's challenging time could be the other's deep, restorative sleep cycle. After both children who are sharing a room are sleeping well and following the same general sleep schedule, it's okay to move them in together. Our preferred method of dealing with siblings is to make the sleep needs of the child not going through sleep teaching a priority. If the child not going through sleep teaching has a difficult time with transitions, we recommend keeping him in his own space so his sleep isn't disrupted and moving the child you are sleep teaching into your room. Then you can move into the living room while you are sleep teaching. If the child not going through sleep teaching is a solid, flexible sleeper, you can move this child into another room (or your room) temporarily while you sleep-teach. If you decide to take this route, make sure you go the extra mile so everyone is comfortable enough to continue this arrangement as long as necessary. Make the move-out fun for your older child and lavish praise for being a helpful big brother or sister.

We realize it may be difficult to give your baby her own sleeping space if you are already space challenged. We work in New York City, and there's not much we haven't seen in terms of cramped quarters. However, we've always been able to come up with a suitable solution—and we know you can too.

If your partner is upset about having to sleep in the living room for a few days, get some blow-up mattresses and foam egg crates and make the living room as comfy as possible. Get each of you some soft new pajamas, eat popcorn, and watch movies like you are having a sleepover. If you're creative, you can change a frustrating time into a fun memory.

Sleep-Teaching Multiples

We highly recommend you figure out a way to separate your multiples during sleep teaching. Even if you want them to share a room in the long term, separating them while they learn to sleep is very helpful. As we discussed in Chapter Two, it's normal for children to wake up in the middle of the night. Since each child learns to sleep in a different way, one child's sleep challenge could make learning an uphill battle for the other.

Our second bit of advice with sleep-teaching multiples is to stagger your start dates and start teaching your more sensitive or challenged sleeper first. If you start with the baby who seems to be more of a challenge, he'll start sleeping sooner, which will make everything much more manageable for you. The other reason is that on some level, you expect your more sensitive sleeper to struggle. Once she can show you she's actually a superstar sleeper, you're going to have the confidence and strength to get your other child on track.

One common assumption is that if one baby's sleep routine isn't awful, it means this child is easygoing or more open to change. That's often, but not always, true. If you happen to start working on the child whose sleep you thought would be easy and find it hard, you could talk yourself out of fixing the other baby's sleep as well.

If you have a sleeper who is supersensitive and another baby who's doing really well, we suggest doing a week of teaching with the first child before starting with the other. And if you have two or more sensitive sleepers and don't want to extend sleep teaching over a month, you can start each child a night apart. This way, both babies will be on the same schedule within twenty-four hours. Just keep in mind that surround-sound crying can make these first few days very intense; try to line up extra help with cooking and cleaning so you can take a nap or go for a walk by yourself.

"If you have twins, even if the other twin is a perfect sleeper, still go through the process with both kids. We didn't do that. Now my twins are nearly four, and Ione, whom we trained, is amazing; she's always ready for bed and a fantastic sleeper now. But Hulton has regressed and always is getting out of bed in the middle of the night."
—TARA AND PAUL C., PARENTS OF IONE AND HULTON

Preparing Toddlers

Four-month-old babies are completely different from those eighteen months and older. The four month old is just starting to roll over, and the toddler is running through your kitchen asking for cookies. Since toddlers are more capable and aware, you should take steps to emotionally prepare them for sleep teaching in ways that would not be necessary for a baby, and examine your own daytime parenting.

Preparing Toddlers Emotionally

Most things in life are easier when everyone is informed and knows what's coming. Unfortunately, your toddler is probably not going to understand if you tell her the new sleep plan. Toddlers learn the best when they can experience something through the eyes of a character. That's why *Sesame Street* is such a valuable program; it has lovable monsters and animals that experience the same situations your toddler is likely to face. As a result, your toddler can store the information away and be somewhat familiar with that situation when it happens to her. But if approximately one week before you plan to start sleep teaching, you present an interesting book and playtime to educate your child about sleep, your toddler will be familiar with the concept of falling asleep on her own.

We have a simple, useful book, *Baby Bear Sleeps*, that we use to help children become familiar with the idea of independent sleep. (The book is available for free downloading on our Web site: www.dreamteambaby.com.) It shows a bear being put to sleep in his crib, waking in the night, going back to sleep on his own, and then getting up in the morning to happy parents. You could also make your own sleep book using stick figures to get your story across. Whether you write your own book or use ours, we recommend you read it several times a day before you start sleep teaching.

You could also check out some sleep-related picture books from the library. The point is that reading some books prior to making changes in your own situation can help your toddler feel much more secure and comfortable with sleep teaching. It gives her a chance to think about sleep in a tangible way and ask questions.

It's often helpful to layer books with dramatic play about sleep. In essence, this gives children a few dress rehearsals before the first night of sleep teaching. Dramatic play does not need to be elaborate. All you need are three toys and a shoebox. You can use dolls, dinosaur figurines, or stuffed animals. Ask your child which ones are the parents and which one is the baby. Then say, "It's bedtime for the baby." The parent figures give the baby figure a hug, and they say, "Baby, we know you like to fall asleep in our arms [or insert whatever negative sleep association you are trying to break], but we know you can fall asleep all by yourself."

Have the mommy and daddy figures hug the baby, put the baby figure in the crib, and then leave the room. Then you stand the baby figure up in the crib and say something to this effect: "Uh-oh! It looks like Baby wants Mommy and Daddy to come rock him to sleep. But Baby remembers that Mommy and Daddy believe that he can do it himself. [Lay the baby figure down, wait a few seconds, and then continue with the story.] Guess what? Baby fell asleep! Hooray for Baby! Baby slept through the night, and Mommy and Daddy woke him up in the morning."

Have the mommy and daddy figures come back and take the baby figure out of the crib and show them hugging the baby. Then say, "Mommy and Daddy are so proud of baby, and they gave him tons of hugs and kisses."

Do these learn-through-play exercises for several days leading up to sleep teaching so your toddler has some time to process the idea of independent sleep. Although your baby may not be mature enough to articulate what is going on, you'll know you planted the message that sleep equals proud parents.

Examine Your Daytime Parenting

The way we parent during the day is pretty much how our child will expect us to parent them at night. If you don't follow through on things related to their behavior during the day, why would your child believe you have similar rules and boundaries at night?

Before you start sleep teaching, it's important to examine how consistent you are with your children during the day. If you're inconsistent, work on changing this behavior before you start sleep teaching.

It's a toddler's job to explore the world around her. A natural part of that includes testing the limits in her world. Your baby isn't intentionally being mischievous; it's just her way of finding out what's negotiable and what isn't. When toddlers have an idea that everything is negotiable, we can't assume they're going to know what to do when a nonnegotiable situation arises. Daytime is a great time to practice because it's when you have the most energy and you're dealing with behavioral situations that you're probably already used to. Once you see that your toddler believes you mean what you say, you can more easily change the deal at night because it isolates the lesson to just sleep. This means drastically less resistance at night, which is nice for everyone.

Whatever consequence you issue during the day, try your hardest to follow through with it. For instance, you might say, "If you throw your book again, then I'm going to take it away." If your son throws the book again, take the book away and explain that you are taking it because you told him not to throw it and he did anyway. Then move on without a lecture. Let your actions do the teaching. Also beware of using hyperbole to scare your kids into listening to you. We've heard parents at the playground say to their misbehaving child, "We're never coming back here if you keep throwing sand." That's a pretty hard one to follow through on. A different way to approach the problem is saying something you can follow through with, like: "We're leaving the playground if you throw sand again."

And if the child throws sand again, simply pack up and explain you're leaving because he didn't listen. Offer compassion when he realizes that park time is over: "Oh, I'm so sorry you're disappointed. Next time, let's not throw sand and maybe we can have a nice long play." Go do something else, and don't rehash the situation; your child will catch on. Setting boundaries doesn't mean you're Cruella De Vil, the villain in *One Hundred and One Dalmatians*. You can be a fun-loving parent and set limits.

> *"It was helpful to check my own parenting during the day. Remember to be more vigilant in demonstrating consistency during the day, when sleep issues occur at night. When I'm consistent all day, my son knows that grown-ups mean what they say."*
> —JILL M., MOM TO ADAM

Prepare Siblings

Sometimes parents are more anxious about how an older sibling will react to their baby brother or sister who is learning how to sleep. Just as we recommend you prepare yourselves for sleep teaching, it's important to plan and prepare your other children for it too.

Here are a few suggestions for making sure your other children aren't too disturbed by sleep teaching:

+ *Plan for the older sibling to spend a weekend away at the home of a close relative or family friend during the initial days of sleep teaching.* If you are lucky enough to have grandparents in the area, the best solution is having your older child spend a Big Girl or Big Boy weekend with them. This way you can get the first few (potentially challenging) days out of the way and give your younger child some extra attention without your older child feeling neglected.

+ *Make your older children feel needed.* Have a conversation with your older children before sleep teaching to explain that their baby brother or sister is "about to learn how to sleep like a big girl or big boy—just like you do." The more help your older children can provide to you and the baby, the more exciting it is to them when the baby does well. So whenever possible involve your older children in the teaching. Here are a few ideas:

- Have them help you color the shoebox that you use as a crib for your child's dramatic play exercises.
- Encourage them to help you play with the baby to keep her awake between naps.
- Have them participate in the wake-up party (we explain what this is in the next chapter).
- Ask questions like, "Your brother has been working really hard to learn how to sleep. What do you think he would like do this afternoon so we can have some fun?"
- Preserve the older child's sleep. Try to keep your older children on track by keeping their sleep schedule consistent and adding a white noise machine to their room. With a white noise machine, your child will snooze peacefully even when there's commotion in the next room.

Prepare Caregivers

As you begin to sleep-teach your baby, you'll want to make sure you have others on the same page when it comes to your plan. This is particularly important for those who complete your circle of child care—your caregivers. To avoid sending your baby mixed messages that could cause confusion and possibly more sleep problems, it will be critical that all of your caregivers try to stay as consistent with your plan as possible.

Babysitters

Many babysitters or nannies are used to running the show. In fact, new parents often rely on the experience of their nannies to teach them how to care for their children. Because your babysitter has a close relationship with your child, she's going to have some strong feelings about how you teach your baby to sleep. It's important to anticipate some of her frustrations and address them thoroughly before you begin.

We recommend discussing the sleep teaching plan with your babysitter and address any questions she may have. Many times a babysitter will nod and agree with you to be polite, so you need to make sure it's clear that your baby will struggle more than necessary if your babysitter is following different rules than you do at night.

If your babysitter has some initial consistency issues, it doesn't mean you need to find a new babysitter, but it does present an opportunity to bring up an important discussion about trust. You're the parent, and you're relying on your babysitter to follow your direction. If you can't trust your employee to do this, what else can't you trust her to do?

In fact, most babysitters adapt, and we created a helpful sleep teaching overview worksheet to help make sure your babysitter understands your expectations and knows exactly how to respond when you're not there (see Appendix B).

Day Care

If your child is in day care, sleep teaching and being consistent during this period can be somewhat challenging. If you can, plan to stay at home the first four days of sleep teaching. Try to take off a day or two of work and start on a long weekend so your baby can get off to a good start, at home, in the perfect napping environment.

Before you start, talk to your day care director about your plans for sleep teaching and how he or she can keep things as consistent as possible for you:

+ *Is the director flexible enough to follow a napping schedule you provide?* If this person can't follow your schedule, is there a consistent napping schedule? If so, you can cross-reference it with the schedules we've provided so you can choose the right bedtime and wake-up time.

+ *Can you bring a lovey?* Most day care facilities will let you bring a lovey. But if for any reason, yours doesn't, it's not a reason to stress. Day care is such a different experience that your baby will most likely not miss it.

+ *Can you provide a white noise machine for the day care facility to use?* Many facilities don't use a white noise machine, and if yours won't let you bring one in, don't sweat it. Like the lovey, your baby will adapt to not having it when she is at day care. Naps may not be "as perfect" as they could be, but it's fine as long as the nighttime sleep is good.

+ *Is there a way to make the nap room darker?* Again, this is a nice-to-have but not a must-have. Some day care facilities don't have the space to have separate rooms for the cribs, and most children will settle down in a brighter space since that is what the other kids are doing in the room.

+ *Are they comfortable putting your baby in the crib awake?* This is the one nonnegotiable. As long as your baby is going into the crib awake for naps, you shouldn't have a problem. But if the providers insist on holding babies until they fall asleep and then putting them in their cribs, you may want to look into another provider.

Night Nurses

Hiring a night nurse or baby nurse to help you when your baby is not ready to sleep through the night can be a great idea, particularly if you're experiencing postpartum depression, have other children, or are back at work. When new parents have too much on their plate and aren't sleeping at night, exhaustion can lead to unsafe sleeping choices. If you find yourself sleeping on your couch at night with your baby who won't settle and your spouse isn't available to help, consider finding another way. Sometimes we just need a good night or two of sleep to stop ourselves from rationalizing an unwise decision.

That said, when you're ready to teach your baby to sleep, we recommend letting your baby nurse go help another family in need. It is your baby nurse's job to change diapers and hold and feed the baby during the night. When it's time to teach your child independence at night, you're going to eliminate the need for diaper changes, holding, and feedings because your baby's going to be sleeping. Everything will change that first night, and we want parents to experience this learning process with their baby. When they do, parents are much more likely to keep sleep on track. They are more consistent and remember how to respond to their baby when there are unexpected bumps in the road.

Friends

Surround yourself with people who believe in you and understand why you're sleep teaching. But try not to invite house guests or host a dinner party during the two weeks of sleep teaching. If a friend is visiting and the two of you have things to do, you might rationalize staying longer at a museum exhibit or going out to lunch a little too close to your baby's naptime.

Relatives

The issues parents face with nannies are similar to what many face with grandparents, but the situation is a bit more complicated. If your parents or in-laws have a different parenting philosophy from you, chances are they'll be resistant to your sleep plan on some level. It's not selfish or malicious. For many reasons, parents constantly seek signs they did an okay job raising their children (us) and hope we agree so much that we'll do what they did. So it's a big blinking "failure" sign if parents see their child choose a different direction.

But don't be afraid of asking your parents for support and involving them. If you're calm and explain to your parents that you love them and need them to be strong to help you be strong, we think they'll come through for you. Could you imagine saying no to your child if she came to you and asked for your emotional strength?

Sweet Dreams!

The final preparation piece for the big day is to make sure you're feeling psyched up and positive. If you start teaching with a noncommittal mind-set (you figure you'll see how it goes), you're setting yourself up for failure. Teaching your child to sleep is complicated, and if you aren't completely ready to do what you need to do to see it through, all you're doing is setting the baby up to cry for no reason. Remember what Master Yoda said: "Do or do not. There is no try." Keep this quote in mind before sleep teaching, and don't start teaching until you're 100 percent confident that you have done everything possible to set your child up for success. If you're pumped up and ready, then turn to Chapter Ten. It's time to learn about the first night of sleep teaching.

Sleep Teaching Took Us from Heartbreak to Happiness

Tami B., mom to Addi

I remember how important it was to believe in my daughter—to believe she was smart, strong, and ready to sleep on her own. It wasn't enough to believe in myself as her mother, although that was important, too. I can remember chanting to myself, "I believe in you, I believe in you," with tears pouring out of my eyes. It truly was a milestone in both of our lives, and witnessing it work was unreal. I felt so proud to be her mommy.

What kept me on track was always remembering that she needs this sleep—and it was the best gift I could give her. Giving her the gift of sleep was no different from giving her good nutrition, fun play, education, and love. It was essential for her growth, her brain, and her development.

One the biggest things I loved about the Dream Team approach was that although there was a specific plan and outline, you also stressed knowing your own child and trusting your gut. As a mom, no statement has been truer than trusting your gut when it comes to your child—and it applied to this process too. I remember you stressing the crib checks—and that I really could go in and check on her as often as I needed to feel comfortable. I felt as if I really didn't want to unless it was urgent because I knew just seeing me would upset my daughter. So I held back from going into her room as much as I could. But on the third day, during naptime, her cry was just different. She just sounded more upset than tired, so I went in immediately, and she had pooped! It sounds like a silly example, but I remember feeling so good because it was as if I reassured myself: I know her—I know her cries, her sounds—and I know when she needs me versus when she needs to cry and sleep.

I also really feel that for me, going through a divorce, having someone there for support was priceless. Everyone needs someone to help them get through this, whether it's a partner, friend, or relative. And it doesn't matter whether it's a phone call, twenty e-mails, fifty text messages, or someone right there holding your hand. You just need to have the support and love of someone. I can honestly say now that I'd be there for anyone going through this—friend or stranger—because at the end of the day, any of us who've had a baby who doesn't sleep can understand each other better than anyone else. So just reach out to someone—a hand, a call, a text—if it helps get you through that hour where you feel that you might give in. That's all that matters. Don't ever be afraid to ask for help.

CHAPTER 10

The First Twenty-Four Hours

You made it! You're finally ready to teach your baby to sleep through the night. Today is "independence day" for everyone in your family. Tonight you're going to reveal to your child that he doesn't need you to go to sleep. This is a monumental moment in your child's life, so approach the day with excitement and a positive attitude.

Keys to Zzzs

- **Make the first day of sleep teaching special.** It's the kick-off event for the entire process.
- **Plan the last nap of the day carefully.** When and how it happens can affect the outcome of either a successful introduction to sleep teaching or a less-than-ideal bedtime experience.
- **Be careful not to overfeed your baby too close to bedtime.** No one wants to go to sleep with an uncomfortably full tummy.
- **Analyze crying according to the roller-coaster model.** Learning to read your baby's cries will help you know when your baby is actually preparing to self-comfort or sleep.

- **Use crib checks when you absolutely feel they're necessary.** But do so only when you're seriously worried about your baby's safety.
- **Don't let your guilt overcome you.** Guilt is a normal feeling. It will go away once you see the positive impact a good night's rest can have on your baby and family.
- **Welcome the morning with a huge wake-up party.** This can be as much fun for you as it is for your baby.

~~~~~~

Imagine sleeping your entire life on a couch and then someone says to you, "Oh, you don't have to sleep there anymore; you can sleep on this comfortable bed." It may be a bit confusing and take some time getting used to sleeping in a new position and having all that space to move around. However, we all know that sleeping in a bed is considerably better than on a couch. While it might feel a little strange the first night, whoever cued you in to that bed really had your best interest in mind.

Remember that analogy. The confidence you would have in recommending a bed over a couch is the same confidence you should have for today. Your child's going to be very happy once the change is made, and so are you. It's an amazing parenting moment when you believe your child can accomplish something and get to witness her doing it.

At this point, ensure you've checked all of these to-dos:

- ☐ Your child is old enough to learn how to sleep on his own.
- ☐ Your child has the ideal safe environment to learn how to sleep.
- ☐ Your child is getting good nutrition during the day.
- ☐ Your child has parents who are on the same team and are committed to being as consistent as possible for at least two weeks.
- ☐ Any older siblings and caregivers have been told that sleep teaching is beginning.

Tonight is when your baby is going to learn to be an independent sleeper, but your job in sleep teaching actually begins the moment your baby rouses for the day. Follow the five steps we have set out next to make sure your baby is absolutely ready for bedtime, and he will be sleeping soundly in no time. Let's get started!

Step 1: Your Daytime To-Do List

+ Plan fun activities.
+ Be sure your baby tanks up. Offer her extra milk and her favorite foods.
+ Plan your child's last nap strategically.
+ Write out the day's schedule.

Plan Fun Activities

The "sleep" part of teaching your baby to sleep doesn't technically start until bedtime today. However, the lesson starts the moment your child starts her day. It doesn't matter what time she wakes up, even if it's 5:48 A.M. What does matter is that when the day starts on the first morning of sleep teaching, you begin it with the same excitement you would if it were her birthday. This is an important tool because it helps to quell any nervousness you may be feeling. Some parents are so nervous about what the end of the day is going to be like that they get lost in themselves. They forget that sleep teaching is about their child, first and foremost—not about themselves. So if you find yourself starting to feel anxious about tonight, take a look in the mirror. Unless you are a professional actor, you'll probably see the anxiety written all over your crinkled brow and tense shoulders. Relax. Shake it off, and focus on the fact that it's your baby's independence day so your happiness comes across as real.

If it were your child's birthday, you'd probably have a little party or, at a minimum, some special activities planned. This day should be no exception. Get your baby out and do something that's fun, stimulating, and age appropriate—perhaps a trip to the zoo or a play date. If you have older kids, perhaps everyone would like a trip to a family restaurant and entertainment center. It doesn't matter if your baby isn't crawling yet. Children love watching other children and mentally capturing their movements to mirror later. If you're lucky enough to have older children, they'll love participating and helping you make this day as fun as possible for their sibling.

Tank Up!

Make sure your child has a full tummy today. That way, you'll worry less about hunger tonight, particularly if he's been used to feeding at night. Here's what we mean:

+ *If your baby is breast feeding,* by now you are probably close to or are succeeding in spacing your feedings during the day to three to four hours apart. We are more concerned about the daytime feedings being spaced properly than the nighttime ones, since your baby's feeding habits are closely related to falling asleep at night. This will be fixed tonight! Even though we ask you to tank up your baby today, resist the urge to cluster breast-feed. Keep your feedings spaced out so that you can make sure your baby is consuming that yummy, fatty hindmilk, and always offer both sides of the breast for each feeding. Even if she has never eaten from both sides in one feeding, offer it anyway. It will give you peace of mind that your baby was satisfied at every feeding today. As a "supply check," you may offer a bottle of expressed breast milk immediately after one or more nursing sessions. If you've been doing a good job at spacing out the feedings, your baby probably won't be interested in the bottle; still, it's a nice exercise to do on the day of teaching. If you're breast feeding, you'll have clear proof that your baby is truly satiated. Remember that a hungry baby won't refuse a bottle.

+ *If your baby is formula-fed (partially or totally),* add two extra ounces of formula to each bottle today. Again, you'll want to make sure your child has had every opportunity to eat as much as he wants throughout the day. Don't worry if your baby doesn't drink the extra ounces. It's a sign he's full, and that will give you the confidence you'll need tonight.

+ *If your child is eating solids,* offer her favorite healthy foods. This way, she'll stay more satiated through the night.

+ *We strongly suggest you restrict all food and liquids for the final hour before sleep teaching.* If your baby is not yet eating solids, your final feed of the day should end no later than thirty minutes before bedtime. This is just for the first two or three nights. A lot of parents are concerned that their baby will wake up hungry in the middle of the night, so they feed right up to the point they put the baby in the crib. In fact your baby needs some time to start digesting before you put him in the crib. Think how hard it is for you to get comfortable right after you eat a big Thanksgiving dinner. In addition, your child is probably going to be frustrated when you put him in the crib. If your baby gets upset on a full belly, it increases the chances she could throw up, especially if she has an easy gag reflex. Nobody wants their baby to get sick, so help her out and do dinner and final milk earlier than usual.

Plan Naps to Your Advantage

When it comes to sleep teaching, you want naps to work to your advantage from the first night of sleep teaching. So ensure your baby is awake for the three to four hours leading up to bedtime:

+ *If your baby is less than six months:* Make sure he is up from his last nap three hours before bedtime.

+ *If your baby is six months or over:* Make sure he is up from his last nap four hours before bedtime.

This means you may have to wake your baby up from his last nap. Sometimes parents feel guilty about this, but they shouldn't feel that way. Being awake for the right amount of time is going to help your baby be optimally tired at bedtime. You want a tired baby at bedtime so he doesn't protest as much when you change the deal. Waking a sleeping child feels very unnatural to a lot of nannies and caregivers, so if you aren't home in the afternoon, check in with them to make sure they've done it.

Possible Nap Scenarios for the Day of Teaching

The No-Napper

Sometimes (although rarely) a child will refuse to nap all day. If that happens, you have two choices: wait one extra day to start sleep teaching so you have another day to make sure your baby naps at least a little or continue with sleep teaching as planned for that night. Both are perfectly fine choices, but there are some drawbacks to each. If you wait an extra day, you may experience a low that makes it harder to achieve your original state of excitement the next day, which may be just enough time to talk yourself out of sleep teaching completely. If you decide to go ahead, dinnertime with an exhausted baby can be challenging, and your baby will most definitely be over-tired by bedtime. You shouldn't worry if your baby has a small dinner or is overtired. You've done a great job just making sure your baby had hearty meals, and most babies are incredibly tired by bedtime the first night. If you decide to proceed, be confident in your decision, and try not to alter the bedtime or let your baby sleep during those final hours before the new bedtime you've chosen.

The Dozer

Some children who are used to controlling when and how they sleep have a hard time staying awake for those final three to four hours leading up to bedtime. If you have a child who keeps nodding off before the official bedtime, do whatever you can to help keep her awake. Avoid cozy walks in the stroller and car trips to the grocery store. Keep her moving. And if nothing else works, give your baby an early bath. Once she feels the water, it might be enough to produce some adrenaline that will keep her going until bedtime.

The I'm-Too-Exhausted-to-Eat-My-Final-Feeding Baby
Don't stress out if the final feeding is paltry. If you did a really good job giving your child great feedings throughout the day, he might not be hungry now. The final feeding is also probably a bit earlier than your child is used to since we moved it ahead, so he may not be as hungry as usual. Either way, if your baby refuses to eat or eats only a fraction of what he normally does during the last feeding, everything is still going to be okay. We all have days when we have larger meals than others, and it's better to believe your baby ate what he wanted than try to stuff him within an hour of bedtime and risk him getting sick.

Create a Schedule for the Day

It's helpful to make a schedule for this day ahead of time so you can ensure you aren't having so much fun that lose track of things and accidentally skip an important step. Here's a good example:

Sample Schedule for a Twelve Month Old

6:30 A.M.	Wake and milk feed
7:30 A.M.	Breakfast
8:00 A.M.	Grandma visit
9:30 A.M.	Milk feed
10:00 A.M.	Trip to museum or take a dip in a community pool

12:00 P.M.	Lunch
12:30 P.M.	Nurse to sleep
3:00 P.M.	Wake up baby (no later than 3:00 P.M.)
3:30 P.M.	Play date at the park
5:15 P.M.	Dinner
6:00 P.M.	Bath
6:30 P.M.	Together time on the couch and reading books
7:00 P.M.	Bedtime—sleep teaching begins!

The bedtime in today's schedule is the same bedtime you chose in Chapter Five. Whichever schedule you've chosen, print it out, and post it on your refrigerator so it will be easy for everyone to follow, starting tomorrow.

Step 2: Your To-Do List for Saying Goodnight

+ Focus on your end-of-day together time.
+ Switch roles and have Dad (or the partner who is not usually in charge of bedtime) put the baby down for bed.
+ Breast-feeding moms pump once at bedtime and a second time before they go to sleep.

Starting Your New Bedtime Routine

Your baby has had a long exciting day, is sweet and clean, fed, and in his jammies. Plan to spend the last twenty to thirty minutes of the day together in a brightly lit "living," not "sleeping," room (especially not the nursery). Choose any of the together time suggestions in Chapter Five: books, songs, massaging, and so on. It really doesn't matter how you choose to connect with your child as long as you aren't propped up on a cozy bed or rocker getting your baby into a sleepy state.

It may feel strange moving your bedtime routine out of the bedroom and not making it overly sleep inducing. But if the routine is quiet, serene, and in a child's sleeping space, it's incredibly easy for a baby to fall asleep during the routine instead of in the crib.

When a child falls asleep with our help, we're starting the work of falling asleep for him. Since you're about to communicate that your baby has the power to put himself to sleep, it's best to remove yourself completely from the falling-asleep process. The way to do this is to stay active until it's time for bed.

Does this sound daunting? Here's your motivation. You've probably just spent the better part of a week getting your baby ready for this night. Bedtime is now approaching. Your baby had a special day and is tired and well fed. There's never been a better moment to teach her how to sleep, and you don't want to risk ruining this special moment by doing anything that does any part of the falling asleep work for her. The reason is that at some point in the night, your baby is going to be fully awake.

But if you've already taught her at bedtime when she's fully awake, she'll have tools when she rouses later in the night. Not only is it easier for her to fall asleep on her own after all the prep work you've done, she'll know what to do when she rouses later and won't feel as dire a need to wait for your help to go back to sleep. Children love sleep as much as we adults do—and once you show them the way, they choose sleep.

A lot of parents are misled by the conventional wisdom that a baby should be put into a crib drowsy but awake, so they think that their bedtime routine is supposed to get the baby into a sleepy state. Drowsy doesn't mean overly tired; it means appropriately tired. If you've had a fun-filled day and followed our guidelines, your child is already drowsy enough for bed. No more work is required, so you can check that off your to-do list.

Time to Say Goodnight

Dad has a very important job waiting for him tonight: he's in charge of putting the baby to bed! The reason for this is threefold. Most babies associate their mom with sleep (which we are trying to break); moms usually log more time taking care of the baby, and at a certain point many dads can feel a little left out; and we like to reel Dad back in and show the entire family that both parents are equally as important and capable.

Now that we've built up your anticipation, here's what we recommend you do when it's time to say goodnight:

1. Finish your together time in the living room. Mom gives lots of hugs and kisses and says goodnight there (channeling her inner Buddha with total calmness).
2. Dad takes the baby into the nursery, closes the blackout shades, changes her diaper, turns on the sound machine, and turns off the light. Mom remains in the living room.
3. Dad walks over to the crib with an awake baby, lays the baby in the crib on her back, hands the lovey to the baby, and says, "Night, night, sweet princess! Daddy loves you very much."
4. Then Dad turns around, walks out the room, and closes the door behind him. (During the first few nights of sleep teaching, turn on a light in the hallway so you don't have to turn a light on in the room if you need to go back in for a crib check.)

Presentation of new bedtime deal accomplished.

You may be asking yourself, *That's it? No pacifier? No swaddle? Not even just a little bit of bouncing?*

Nope. The simpler your routine for placing your child in his crib, the easier it will be for him to have the tools he needs to recreate the same conditions in the middle of the night.

"Breast-feeding moms need to be wary of keeping up their supply because their nighttime feeding schedule may change dramatically. This doesn't mean that you need to wake up and express on your usual

schedule. On the contrary, we want you to sleep. The best way to help your body adjust is by planning to pump three times. First, pump off excess supply immediately after the baby goes to bed. Second, pump right before you go to bed so your breasts are comfortable and empty. That way, you can get some much-needed consolidated sleep and wake up with nice and full breasts so your baby can get the feeding of a lifetime when he rouses in the morning. Third, pump right after your first feeding of the day. Supply is the greatest in the morning after all that good sleep, and pumping now will help kick start more daytime production."

—CAROLYN MIGLIORE, LACTATION CONSULTANT

Step 3: Handling Nighttime Issues

+ Listen to the cries.
+ Learn to deal with rousings.
+ Use crib checks for unusual crying or concerns.
+ Use a one-time pass for teaching moments.
+ Respond consistently.

Listen to the Cries

Now it's time to readdress the very large elephant in the room.

Let's assume your child isn't immediately on board with this new routine. We would really love you to prepare yourself for the fact that your baby will cry when confronted with this change. Change in fact is frustrating for all of us, including babies. And just to set up your expectations before reading this section, at no point are we going to say that it's okay to ignore your baby if he's crying. Still, we are going to teach you how to figure out when something is wrong and your baby needs you versus the times your baby is working on something and needs some space.

Here's what to do. When Dad leaves the nursery, listen to what is happening before you react. Think of your baby's cries as if they were a foreign language. Being around people who are speaking a language you don't understand can be uncomfortable and upsetting. They could be talking about something as innocent as a mistake the dry cleaner made, but if they really loved that red dress the dry cleaner ruined, it could sound really scary. If you don't know what's being communicated, it's easy to misinterpret the situation based on intensity and volume alone.

Unfortunately, since many young children don't have the ability to form words yet, the only sounds they make when they're frustrated are crying sounds. These sounds are particularly excruciating for their parents to hear. Before we begin working with some clients, they say their baby screams nonstop, sometimes for hours at a time. And yes, if you're paying attention only to the high points of a cry, it *can* sound like continuous screaming. But not all crying is saying the same thing. That's why we tell parents to pay attention to the highs and lows within a baby's cries.

For instance, when babies are frustrated, they can't help themselves from crying, but they are tired and want to gain their composure at the same time. This tug of war causes the crying to get louder and then softer and then loud again and then softer. The softer moments are those times when your baby's doing some really good work to calm down.

Most children will not require your assistance from the very point that you walk out of the nursery, so listen carefully. After what is perhaps an initial unwavering wail, you should soon hear the ups and downs of the crying. This is a good example of an "I'm frustrated" cry.

Assuming that nothing goes wrong and that your baby is just fine (if frustrated in that moment), you can expect her to go through several phases of learning before the initial falling asleep moment.

We like to think of it as a hill or a roller coaster, with the numbers in this list corresponding to the numbers in the illustration:

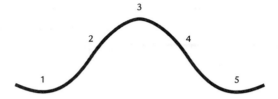

1. At first, the baby cries to say, "Uhhhhh, excuse me please! You put me here in this crib, but you forgot to nurse me to sleep!"
2. Next, the baby raises the volume. "Hello! I'm really tired! You left me here completely awake and I *need* to go to sleep!"
3. Then the crying gets even harder when the baby realizes this doesn't seem to be helping—and may even give it one more supercharged cry just to see why crying isn't getting her what she wants.
4. The baby begins to remember she's tired and realizes she's going to have to take matters into her own hands, though she's not sure how yet. As she considers the options, she accidentally sucks her thumb (or rubs her feet, bites her lovey, or something else) a few times and feels better. As she feels better, these actions will become more deliberate; you will know this is happening because these moments of soothing are going to sound to you like pauses.
5. The baby has completely calmed herself down and is working toward sleep.

Learn to Deal with Rousings

Phase 3 is the time when a lot of babies give it their all. It's difficult to listen to their frustration, but it's often necessary to get to the soothing phases. Once your baby enters phase 4 and starts to experiment with calming himself down, you should start to hear pauses of silence interspersed within the frustration, though this won't be perfect right away. These pauses may be only five seconds long, but even this short intermission is a very good sign. As your baby gets better and better at calming down, these pauses become more frequent and longer in duration, until finally your baby succeeds—reeling in any lingering frustration in order to do what feels right in the moment—by falling asleep.

Your baby will go through several sleep cycles that cause her to rouse in the middle of the night. When she does rouse, try not to let it get you down. We like to think of these arousals as learning opportunities. Each time your baby triumphs and falls asleep, even just for a while, is a huge accomplishment!

Some babies sleep very well through morning sleep transitions, while other babies will have a harder time in the early morning than at bedtime. Both reactions are normal. Your goal the first night is to get your baby to the wake-up time without resorting to any of the old negative sleep associations.

Checking On Your Baby

All babies' personalities are different. Their history with learning to sleep is different, and their cries are different. This is one reason we don't like to prescribe specific, timed check-ins or put a specific time limit on crying during the night. We also don't like hard-and-fast rules because we want to encourage you to listen and learn what it sounds like when your baby truly needs you. That's why we have you listen for the ups and downs, for the gradual increase, and then the subsequent coming down once your baby starts working on self-soothing. Hearing your child go through these phases is key, because you will be able to learn how to differentiate his normal and frustrated cries.

In no way are we suggesting that you just lie in your bed and listen to your baby cry all night. Sometimes your baby may legitimately need your help. If you're focusing on listening, you will know when you hear something unusual. If you are ever concerned about your child, perform what we call a crib check.

Here's how to decide whether you should do a crib check so it has the least impact on your child's learning process:

1. Listen for the pauses and the lows in the cries.
2. If you hear a different-sounding cry that makes you feel your baby's safety or health is in danger, go in and do a crib check.
3. If the highs and lows are continuing but you start to feel a strong desire to check on your baby, set a timer for five minutes. Before you go in, try to wait the full five minutes.
4. If your child has stopped crying or is calm by the time the five minutes is up, do not go into the nursery. However, if your child starts crying again and you feel that you need to know she's okay, feel free to perform a crib check.

A crib check is meant to be exactly that—a check to see if your baby's in trouble. If possible, we recommend Dad do these checks the first few nights. But whoever does them should channel their inner firefighter. Everyone likes firefighters, but few come to the rescue and offer hugs when nothing is wrong. They show up, survey the scene for an emergency, and then leave. If firefighters were known for giving hugs as well as saving people from burning buildings in response to 911 calls, we suspect they would be much busier. A crib check should take thirty seconds or less if nothing is wrong.

Here are the steps to doing a proper crib check:

1. Make sure there's a light on in the hallway so when you enter, you don't have to turn on a light in the room.
2. Enter the room calmly so your child doesn't feel as if this is an exciting visit.
3. Be completely neutral and unemotional when you're in the room. That means you are focused on sticking to the facts and not interacting at all: no talking, no eye contact, and no picking

up your baby unless absolutely necessary. If you do any of these things, you could inadvertently send a message to your child that says, "Cry really hard and I'll come in eventually and reward you with some attention." Attention, whether it's negative or positive, can be a reward, and it's best not to encourage your child to rely on you when she's capable of falling asleep on her own.

5. Check for anything that may need your attention (again, picking up the baby only if absolutely necessary): poopy or leaking diapers, entrapment in crib slats, illness, or the most common culprit, a false alarm. If you find something's wrong, quickly fix it without talking or showing signs of emotion. If nothing's wrong, leave the room quietly and calmly without saying a word.

After you leave the room prepare for a temporary escalation in frustration. Going in likely raised your baby's expectations that this new deal was off. As such, it is humanly reasonable that your child will be more frustrated than before your crib check. Don't let this temporary escalation make you avoid doing a crib check and ignore your instinct. We tell parents all the time that it's better to know your baby is okay than to ignore your instincts because you were scared your baby would be angry if nothing ended up being wrong.

Plus, ignoring your instincts is anxiety provoking and can cause you to lose focus. Even if you have to do crib checks every ten minutes all night long because you are nervous, it's better than going in and nursing for two minutes, for example. Although a crib check is better than giving in to a negative sleep association, we don't recommend checking this frequently. It can set your baby up for expecting a visit, which could communicate that something is wrong or distract him from going to sleep.

Over the coming days (and after you have several falsely pulled emergency alarms under your belt), both you and your baby will become more familiar with the times she needs you and the times she just needs to sleep. If you are listening to the crying, it'll sound different and you'll know very clearly when something is wrong.

"Trust your maternal instinct when listening to the cries. I really have learned to distinguish when the cry is just an 'I-don't-want-to-be-sleep-trained' cry versus something being wrong or someone being sick. It's always hard to hear your baby cry, but when you know that nothing is seriously wrong and your baby is safe, it makes the process much easier!

—ALLYSON F., MOM TO OLIVER AND CHASE

"When you told us to wait another five minutes before going in, we did that, and our daughter almost always stopped crying before the five minutes was up. I have only had to go into her room maybe three times in the fifteen months since you helped us."

—AMY M., MOM TO MARLIE AND CHRISTIAN

"It's important to wait the extra five minutes before doing a crib check because many children give crying their all just before they calm down. The technical term is an extinction burst: it's a temporary increase in behaviors that have previously been reinforced. It's a last effort to see if parents are really serious about this new limit they've set, similar to when you stand at an elevator that isn't working and keep pressing the button to make it work. You realize it doesn't help and you stop pressing it. If you stay calm and stick to your checks without giving in, it's often the turning point in changing a behavior."

—BRITT MOORE, CHILD BEHAVIORIST

Use a One-Time Pass for Teaching Moments

Sometimes when parents hear an unusual cry, they do a crib check and discover their child has just reached a milestone in the crib. For example, he may have rolled over on his belly for the first time and is feeling a bit disoriented. Or he has pulled himself up and doesn't know how to get down. It's very exciting, but your child may be a bit confused because now he feels different. Children commonly hit a milestone in the middle of learning to sleep. They begin getting more sleep, which means better-rested minds and bodies, both of which contribute to development.

How you respond when your child learns a new physical skill is critical to maintaining the healthy sleep habits you are creating. We suggest you use what we call a one-time pass to teach your child he has the skills to deal with whatever surprise he encounters. You want to show your baby how to get out of the trap. If your baby is sitting up, you can carefully move his shoulders down so he is lying down again. If your baby is standing up, you can take his hands and let him bend his knees until he sits or lies down.

Show your baby what to do without lifting your child up and placing her in a position. If you lift your child, you are doing something she cannot do herself, which can communicate that she needs you when she is in this new position. And that will distract her from figuring out that she can do it on her own.

Once you show your baby what to do, it's his job to do it the next time. Remember that all of these small moments can have a major impact on your child's sleep. If you respond and react when your baby truly doesn't need you, you can confuse your child about where the boundary lies, which means your baby will have more "questions" that manifest in the form of more crying at night.

Never underestimate how much your child trusts you. Children look to us for cues about what they can and can't do. If your baby can get on her belly, she needs to learn to sleep on her belly. If your baby can sit up, she needs to close her eyes and lie down. Although your child has a new skill, she still has the capacity to sleep. The more relaxed you are about that, the more relaxed your baby will be. In addition, once she does it, you'll become a hero because you believed in her when she didn't believe in herself—and that's how trust is built.

Consistency Is Key!
This whole method is created on the foundation of consistency:

- Consistent environment
- Consistent schedule
- Consistent response
- Consistent belief

Consider this situation from clients who were in the middle of sleep teaching. Their baby had done extremely well the first few days—only one very brief rousing in the middle of the night. But on day 4, the baby woke unexpectedly in the early morning. Instead of doing a crib check, the dad changed the baby's wet diaper (which wasn't necessary), hoping it'd help the baby go back to sleep. Just that tiny unnecessary interaction opened up a window that was previously closed. It gave the child enough hope that someone might come back. So instead of going back to sleep as he had done the other nights, he was awake and crying for an extended period of time before his scheduled wake-up time.

This father rationalized an impulse instead of weighing the consequences. Just this one incident of inconsistency set the sleep teaching back. A better course of action would have been that when the baby woke at 5:30 A.M., Dad stayed in bed and listened. If the cry was a normal up and down, he could feel confident the baby was just learning how to go back to sleep after ten hours of sleep. But if the crying escalated, the baby wasn't able to calm down, or if Dad felt that something was off, he could have done a crib check to survey the scene. Seeing that everything was fine, he'd quickly leave and the baby would likely calm down, similar to any other rousing in the middle of the night.

"The key thing I learned was this: the best way to ensure a behavior continues is to react to it. This made so much sense. Not just in sleep training, but in parenting in general. I still apply this rule now during the terrible two's."
—KRISTEN H., MOM TO LILAH

Step 4: Believe in Your Baby

Parents tell us all the time their child seems to hate her crib or doesn't attach to anything other than her mom. But these so-called sleep problems generally stem from a miscommunication of sorts between parent and child. The baby has very little to do with the problem; she's just following her parents' lead.

Common First Night Issues

Each baby's reaction to sleep teaching is different. Some babies adapt with relative ease and some struggle more than their parents anticipate. Your baby's initial reaction is not always indicative of how quickly he will learn to sleep.

Understanding the most common kinds of reactions to sleep teaching will help you maintain composure because you'll understand why your baby might struggle at certain times. It'll also help you be more patient and proud of your baby's progress as she overcomes these challenges.

Trouble Falling Asleep at Bedtime

If your baby has always been put down for the night already asleep and has gone through several attempted rounds of failed sleep training efforts, he might will himself to stay awake because he knows you are going to change your mind. Once he realizes he's going to have to do it on his own, falling into a deep sleep can be hard work. He may struggle for a while, fall asleep for a brief time, and then wake up again shortly after to give it another shot in case you'll change your mind—and then go to sleep. You might hear this baby again in the morning, but the cries are usually much different—more as if he's trying to go to sleep on his own instead of waiting for you. Listen for cues that he's settling; do your crib checks if necessary to ensure everything's okay.

Falls Asleep Easily But Wakes One to Three Hours Later to Protest
Some parents have done such a good job getting their baby ready for bedtime that she doesn't even cry when they put her down awake. Don't be fooled! This baby hasn't had a chance to catch on yet that the deal has changed. Whether she rouses forty-five minutes or six hours later, this is the moment for learning. Be mentally prepared for it; then listen to the cries and do crib checks if necessary. Some parents can talk themselves into rationalizing giving in with thoughts like, "She woke because she was hungry. She didn't take much of her last bottle." But if you did your feeding homework, got your pediatrician's approval, and did a "tank-up" day, she won't be starving. Let your baby do the work to get to sleep. Once you know she was aware of what she did to fall asleep, you'll know her sleep will start to improve if you're consistent.

Super-Hungry Baby
We know your baby is ready to sleep through the night if you did your feeding homework, your baby is growing along his growth curve, and your baby is at least four months old, gestationally corrected. But we also understand you may not believe it's possible for your child to go without at least one feeding the first night of sleep teaching. Although we highly recommend you trust that your baby can do this, we don't want you to feel disheartened if your maternal instinct is urging you to feed your baby. If this is the case, follow these steps:

- **Keep this feeding all business.** The objective of a feeding during sleep teaching is to give your baby a tide-me-over until the first morning feeding, not to stuff your baby. We want your baby to transfer her calorie consumption to daytime, and the best way to do that is to have a hearty first feeding of the day. Any calories you give your baby at night will affect how enthusiastic she is for this feeding after waking up.
- **Stretch your baby at least six hours.** A three-month-old baby can go at least six hours without a feeding at night, so this

uld not feel too lofty a goal and will get you through several
major sleep cycles.

**If your baby rouses after the six-hour mark (but before the
nine-and-a-half-hour mark), you can give your baby a feeding.**
We recommend a bottle feeding (breast milk or formula) and
no more than four ounces. If you are breast feeding and have
never before given a bottle to your child, limit the feeding to five
minutes.

- **If your baby rouses between nine-and-a-half to eleven hours,
  we recommend offering a little less.** For this feeding, we suggest
  offering no more than two ounces from a bottle (breast milk or
  formula). If you are breast feeding and have never before given
  a bottle to your child, limit the feeding to three minutes.

- If your baby rouses between eleven and twelve hours, we recommend that you try to wait until wake-up to feed your baby.

- **We recommend standing up during these feedings in the
  nursery.** If you have to sit down, have a kitchen chair available
  in the room instead of your cozy rocker. If you can keep this
  feeding all business (hence the standing or sitting in a not-so-
  comfy chair), you'll see whether your baby wanted a feeding for
  comfort or if she is truly hungry.

- **If your baby resists eating, end the feeding.** A hungry baby will
  eat, and a baby looking for something else (say, to satisfy a
  negative sleep association) will not be all that interested.

- **Once you are done, put your baby back in the crib awake and
  let him fall asleep on his own.** Because you offered a feeding,
  expect that your baby will want that feeding the next night, but
  resist the temptation to keep offering it night after night, or it
  will delay the learning process.

Early-Morning Wakings

Some babies may work very hard to go to sleep but wind up doing
pretty well once they're down. Often the problem for these children

comes in the early morning—about the time their stomachs start to feel a little empty. If your baby is used to getting a feeding as soon as he wakes in the morning, he's most likely going to ask for one. Since we assume you did a great job with your feeding homework, remind yourself that you have a healthy baby and a few extra hours before a feeding will be okay. If you hold off, your baby's first feed will be very hearty, and he'll probably eat more than usual, helping to shift those old nighttime feedings to the daytime. If your baby hasn't been eating in the middle of the night but still wakes early, the reason is most likely he just got ten or eleven hours of sleep. And although that isn't enough sleep, it's probably a lot better than what he was getting before. Now the challenge for him is to learn to go back to sleep when he's somewhat rested.

Difficulty On and Off, All Night Long
Some babies have willpower. It's a great quality but can shake parents' confidence during sleep teaching. A baby who seems to cry on and off all night is really uncommon, but there are certain babies who have to work through every challenge:

- Falling asleep from being awake
- Waking in the crib and learning to put herself to sleep
- Rousing again in the early morning because she could be used to being fed
- Rousing again at the ten- or eleven-hour sleep transition

This type of learner is both the hardest and easiest—hard because it can feel as if she's crying on and off all night long and easier because she's actually consolidating her learning, so she catches on fast. That's because she had so many opportunities to wake and fall asleep the first night, she's often a seasoned veteran after only a night or so. If you start to get the feeling that your baby is this kind of learner, it's helpful to have a pad of paper so you can record all of the sleeping periods. That way, you'll be able to remind yourself she's actually getting some sleep. These babies are hard to be strong for, because it feels as if the night will never end. Hug your partner a lot, and don't forget to do your crib checks to fix anything that's amiss or reassure yourself that everything's okay. Once you can get to the wake-up time, you're set because the next night will be amazing!

Coping with Crying

We know it's hard to turn off your impulses and emotions when you hear your child cry, but we urge you to manage your stress during this time. The more stressed you are, the more stressed your baby will be, which is going to make it much harder for him to relax into sleep when you put him in his crib.

If you find yourself near your breaking point, here are a few strategies for remaining calm during bouts of frustrated crying:

- Take a relaxing bath.
- Enjoy a glass of wine.
- Put on calming music.
- Journal about how you are feeling.
- Take twenty deep breaths.
- Get a huge hug from your spouse.
- Let your spouse listen to the baby while you go for a walk around the block.
- Have a calming friend come over to help during the process.
- Look back on your "Why We're Teaching Our Child to Sleep" list.
- Become your baby's cheerleader; talk to yourself as if you were talking to your baby: "Come on Charlotte, you can do it! Come on, sweet girl! Great pause! You're getting there!"

In the long run, giving your child space to figure it out on her own will help her become more independent. There aren't any convincing studies that prove allowing your child to cry during sleep teaching diminishes a child-parent connection.

dream team

"Sleep teaching is consistent with being a caring parent. You care so much for your child that you're willing to tolerate the temporary discomfort of crying for the long-term gain of a healthy sleeper."

—DR. AMY DEMATTIA, PEDIATRICIAN

"Everyone will say, 'Don't give up,' and as easy as it is to say, it isn't that easy to do. You will hear your baby cry, and what is only five minutes of crying seems like three hours to a parent, but it will eventually click."

—JENNIFER C., MOM TO MICHAEL

If you're worried your child won't fall asleep tonight, run through this list to make sure you haven't missed anything:

- Is your baby over four months?
- Is your baby healthy and approved for sleep teaching?
- Is your baby well fed?
- Is your baby on an age-appropriate schedule?
- Is your baby in a crib in a dark room at a temperature of between sixty-eight and seventy-two degrees with a white noise machine?
- Is your baby's room safe, and is the crib free of any toys or large blankets that might pose a risk?

- Did you put your baby in the crib awake after he was awake for three or four hours, depending on his age?
- When you were concerned something was wrong, did you wait five more minutes, make sure nothing was wrong, and if so, leave the room in a quiet, neutral way?

If all of your answers to these questions are yes, there's no reason that your baby cannot learn to be an independent sleeper.

This is your baby's journey, and your job is to be a steady rock for her while she's learning how to sleep. If you aren't in the game and focused, your mind can actually talk you out of believing your child is ready.

We worked with a mom who was certain her son was scared in his room. She'd sit and reassure him everything was okay every time he called out in the night. But instead of making him more comfortable, her presence made the problem worse. The child had a very stable and safe home life, and there was no real cause for the fears.

Why did it get worse, not better, with his mom in the room? Every time his mom rushed in, she was communicating to her son that she believed there might in fact be a reason to be scared. Through some digging, we discovered that the mom remembered being afraid of the dark when she was young and was allowed to sleep with her grandmother to feel better. So we went through the facts with her and helped her arrive at the conclusion that the house and room were totally safe. Once she looked inward and truly believed there was nothing for her son to be afraid of and remained composed during the night, the fear fests ended within twenty-four hours.

We're all far from perfect. Whether we like it or not, we bring our issues into the way we care for our children. However, our baggage can sometimes prevent us from being the kind of parents we want to be. If we don't keep our own feelings in check, it can sometimes stop us from doing the best thing for our kids.

We don't want to send you into a deep, downward spiral of introspection. That's not why we brought it up. But lack of sleep, hearing a baby cry, and seeing your child frustrated or struggling can trigger issues you didn't know existed.

We may feel guilty about working during the day, so we cave to our child's "need" for nighttime attention. Or maybe you suffered several miscarriages, did in vitro fertilization, and worked so hard to have this baby that you made a pact to never make this baby suffer. All of these feelings are completely normal, and that's really why we're here to help you. It's hard work being a parent—and it can be hard learning to separate instinct or emotion from fact.

"The excuses we were pinning on Hunter for not sleeping were actually our excuses as parents for not having the trust in Hunter to learn to sleep by himself. We needed to be confident in Hunter in order for him to be confident in himself to put himself to sleep and stay asleep."
—HALLE G., MOM TO HUNTER

Step 5: Wake-up! Time to Celebrate!

If you look at your schedule, there is a scheduled wake-up time for the day. That time is your goal, so try not to start your day twenty minutes or five minutes before it; give your baby an opportunity to fall back to sleep and get the bonus sleep. If she's awake at the wake-up time, you can go in and start the day. If she's asleep, you can let her sleep until the bonus thirty minutes are up.

Whether your child is awake or asleep, gather everyone in the house and go in to kick off the day on a positive note: hosting the first of many wake-up parties to come.

You'll always do some version of a wake-up party when you get your baby up from the nighttime sleep (you'll do it for naps, too; more on that in the next chapter). Essentially whoever's in your house at a wake-up point joins in for a joyous welcome from the land of sleep to the land of awake (and fun!). Some parents really get into the party and bring in siblings, hats, and even posters. You don't need to go all out with balloons and conga lines, but do get your energy up.

Here's the reason this is such a critical step. There's a pretty good chance your baby's a little confused by the events of the night. It's up to you to communicate that what transpired was a good thing and he did a good job.

Before you go into your baby's room to get her up for the day, check yourself out in a mirror. Look carefully at your face and smile. Check your partner and make sure there are no signs of stress in his or her body either. Your child doesn't have the capacity to understand the emotional complexities of parenting, and the last thing she needs to think is, "Poor Mommy. I wonder if I made her sad?" Go into your child's room, wake her if you need to, and give her a huge hug and a huge smile. Let your baby know all's well by kissing and hugging her, and telling her you're so proud of all the hard work she did the night before.

The wake-up party turns this sometimes difficult learning period into a positive one. If you're happy, you're going to make your baby smile—and once you see your baby smile, you'll both know everything's going to be okay.

"Don't underestimate the power of a wake-up party! At first it seemed silly for us to celebrate my daughter's waking, especially if it had not been a great night or nap. But we figured we had nothing to lose. My husband went so far as to make up a wake-up party song and made a big production every morning. Now seven months later, my daughter looks forward to the fun that awaits her in the morning after a good night's sleep, and she even asks for the party. It's helped us motivate her to sleep better when we've been sidelined with illness and other sleep disruptions."

—DAN AND JULIE M., PARENTS OF KIRA

Sweet Dreams

Learning and adapting to change can be a strain on both parents and babies, but with the right amount of cooperation, communication, and cheerleading, anything's possible. It's important to break down the old routines in order to establish healthier (and probably less time-consuming) ones. You're all on your way to better sleep!

CHAPTER 11

The Next Two Weeks
(Including Naps)

I t's hard to commit to anything for two weeks, much less something you've never done before. You knew sleep teaching would be a two-week process and were game before it started, but now that you're a day into the process, you may be having second thoughts about sticking it out. That's a normal way to feel, particularly if the first night was tough. Two weeks might seem like a very long time right now. But if you're about to throw in the towel, we urge you to stay totally consistent and give it two more days. We think you'll see some progress by then and have renewed motivation to keep things going.

Keys to Zzzs

- **Bite off a smaller piece if you're struggling.** It's better to succeed in smaller steps than feel as if you're failing in the entire sleep teaching process.

- **Prepare yourself mentally for the first nap of the day.** It will get you in the right mind-set for helping your baby learn to love sleep.

- Recognize that naps are sometimes the biggest challenge for sleep teaching parents. It helps to know you're not alone.
- Know where you should and shouldn't make changes in the schedule or your overall plan. Some things will work for you as they are, while others may need to be modified as you teach your baby to love sleep.
- Remember that for most sleep teaching problems, there are solutions. It's not as hopeless as it may sometimes feel.

If you've started teaching, your child has already put in some hard work. The most learning (and often the most frustration on everyone's part) will happen in the first three days of sleep teaching. It's going to get easier after that point. We hope that your baby's progress over those days will give you the courage and strength to keep going for the full two weeks. But if after three more days, you're feeling defeated, we suggest you try out some of the troubleshooting options at the end of this chapter before you give up entirely.

How do you know if the sleep teaching is or isn't working? It may not be predictable, because when it comes to sleep, a child's progress can be cyclical. As babies get better sleep at night, naps may become harder because babies aren't as tired. When naps get easier, nighttime may become harder for your child because he isn't so tired at bedtime. Rest assured, though, progress is being made, and as the two weeks pass, sleep will get better and better.

If you need more encouragement, look back at Chapters Seven and Eight. Pull out your sleep contract and read all of the reasons you decided to embark on this journey, or call a friend for moral support. Remind yourself that sleep is a wonderful gift to give your child, and you're a good parent for trying.

Naps

If you picked up this book because you're trying to fix a napping problem, chances are you skimmed the previous chapters and skipped directly to this one. And who can blame you? We like to be efficient too. But even if your child's nighttime sleeping is "good enough," it's not a great idea to follow our guidelines for naps if you haven't made modifications to nighttime sleep too. The reason is that nighttime is when it's easiest for children to learn a new way of sleeping. It may seem easier to deal with naps in the moment, but that'll generally be harder on your child.

Difficulty with naps can indicate a crack in nighttime sleep, so it's best to look at the whole picture. We've discovered certain babies are naturally good nighttime sleepers, even if their nighttime sleeping situation has some negative sleep associations. Although these sleep obstacles can go unnoticed at night, they often rear their heads during daytime and make naps more difficult. If your baby can learn to be an independent sleeper at night, he'll be far more likely to have the tools necessary to fall asleep for naps when it's time. If you go the extra mile and make the changes recommended in Chapter Ten before working on naps, both you and your child will be ready for any challenge ahead.

Still not convinced? Parents call us every day looking exclusively for nap help. But no matter the circumstance, we always start their child's teaching at bedtime.

Preparing Mentally for Naptime After the First Night

Congratulations! Your baby just graduated from her first night of independent sleeping. We hope you celebrated this accomplishment with an amazing wake-up party. You may be tired and stressed, but kicking off the day on an optimistic note helps reset everyone's mood to the positive.

After the wake-up party, move on with your day as if everything's totally normal. Feed and play with your child, and if he's on the young side (under twelve to fifteen months), remember the first nap is coming up soon, so you can be as relaxed and confident as possible.

If you feel yourself starting to get nervous, pull your shoulders up toward your ears, release them down your back, and take a deep breath. Remind yourself that all you're doing is asking your child to fall asleep on her own. If your baby is at least four months old (gestationally corrected), there's no reason to doubt her competence.

Sleep teaching can be hard work for you too. Just try to keep that a secret from your baby. The last thing you want to do is communicate that you are struggling. She could interpret that to mean that you aren't happy with the hard work she did the previous night. Try to muster some strength (and perhaps hone your acting chops). How will you handle the heartbreak when a boy breaks your teenage daughter's heart some day? Will it break your heart too? Absolutely. But will you show it? No, because you also know that what your daughter needs is a strong, supportive parent who has perspective and can give her reassurance. Teaching sleep is sometimes the first moment for parents when they have to be strong so their child can learn good coping skills. As the days go on, you'll see what an amazing job your baby is doing, which should affirm all your work and make being positive even easier.

Show your child you are feeling positive and proud. Reward his work by planning some special activities. Of course, make sure he's close to home, so you can get him back in time for naps.

"My Dream Team consultant told me to listen for 'the lows' in the crying when I was sleep training Owen, explaining this was an indication he was learning. This made a big difference to me and reinforced the idea that I was doing something active to help my child learn how to sleep, as opposed to something passive that was benefiting only me. The idea I hang on to with so many parenting challenges is that this is *often a 'pay now' or 'pay later' endeavor. I chose to pay now and teach both my children, Owen and Grace, to sleep while they were infants, as opposed to delaying the inevitable battles that will come when they're older and so much more resistant to changes in their expectations. When people would ask me how I could bear to listen to them cry, I was confident that a few nights of crying during sleep training doesn't even begin to approach the amount of crying an overtired child with poor sleep habits experiences daily, with no end in sight!"*

—RACHEL B., MOM TO OWEN AND GRACE

Following the New Sleep Schedule

Try very hard to stick to your new schedule right away, resisting the temptation to ease into sleep teaching. Despite what you think, being relaxed with the schedule will generally not make it easier for your baby. Think about your schedule as a dance to music that you've never heard before. At first, it will feel a little clumsy, but if you keep listening and dancing, your body will be able to predict notes and follow in sync. The schedule is one of your keys to helping your baby relax into sleep. If you follow it exactly, your baby's body will adjust to when things should be happening and start to prepare itself for the next task. We've heard from clients that they don't have to think about time after a while because their baby knows the schedule better than they do.

The schedules we suggested have a method to their madness. Putting down your child early or late for a nap can sometimes be problematic during these first two weeks. For some babies, being five minutes late for a nap is not a problem. But for others, timing is everything—and being five minutes late for a nap can mean thirty minutes of crying versus no crying. Be sure to keep your schedule close at hand so you don't accidentally get off track.

As you start following your feeding and sleeping schedule, there are two key things to keep in mind:

+ Milk feedings are scheduled immediately after waking. This will help reinforce that they don't always need a completely full stomach to fall sleep.

+ Milk feedings are separated from solids to encourage your child to maximize feedings. This will also ensure that your baby is optimizing the nutrition received from both milk and solid feedings.

The feeding schedules provided in this book are only a guide. They work well for most parents, but not necessarily for everyone, so it's okay if you need to tweak the feedings a little earlier or later. You know best how to manage all the parts in your life. However, now that you are teaching your child to sleep, try to follow the suggested sleeping schedules in this book as closely as possible. If your baby seems to be struggling, read on for some possible variations to the schedule.

Even if you have to make a little variation to the schedule, try your hardest to stick to the full nap and nighttime sleep times for at least the first two weeks. It'll allow you to see the potential of the great little sleeper inside your child and ensure that your child gets the maximum amount of sleep possible. And once your child is a great sleeper, it'll be much easier to relax a schedule than to increase the duration of sleeping times.

Tips for Mastering Naps

Even great nappers can often take ten to fifteen minutes to fall asleep; they'll sleep for thirty to forty minutes, rouse a bit, and then put themselves back to sleep for another cycle of nap sleep. Here are a few reminders and guidelines to help keep you on track during naps:

+ *Use the same sleep environment for naps as for nighttime sleep.* The room is dark, the room temperature is between sixty-eight and seventy-two degrees, white noise is on, and a lovey is in the crib—the same as at night. With these surroundings, your baby will be more likely to recognize that it's time to sleep.

+ *Avoid catnaps outside the crib.* We know it will be hard at first, but beware of the catnap. Even a two-minute snooze in the stroller can ruin a nap that your baby still needs and will be much more restorative in the long run.

+ *Babies should be completely awake when put to bed.* Naps are opportunities to recharge throughout the day, but they're also another chance for your baby to learn to calm herself down and make the choice to sleep.

+ *Limit continuous crying to no more than one hour.* When it comes to learning during the daytime, your baby has a shorter amount of time to attempt a nap before it's time to wake up again. If your child protests, try your very best to give him one hour to fall asleep before you declare the nap officially over.

+ *For a two-hour nap, the same recommendation applies.* Do not let your baby cry continuously for more than one hour. For instance, if your child protests for fifteen minutes, sleeps for thirty minutes, and then wakes up, she still has more than an hour left in her scheduled nap. In this case, we recommend giving her an hour to fall back asleep. If she doesn't go back to sleep, abandon the nap. If she does fall asleep, then the "no more than one hour of continuous crying" resets. The nap is over whatever comes first: the hour of continuous crying or the official end of the nap. For example, if she wakes up with forty-five minutes left in the nap, let her try to get back to sleep for forty-five minutes (that is, when the nap is officially over).

+ *Use crib checks when needed.* Your child is likely going to get more, not less, upset when she sees you, so you want to limit crib checks during naps to when you think something is really awry. When you go in, make the check short, sweet, and boring.

+ *Always end with a wake-up party.* For each opportunity you give your child to learn to sleep independently, whether nighttime or naptime, top it off with a wake-up party. This happy, well-defined transition from sleep time (devoid of stimulation or parental interaction) to awake time (full of light, colors, and excited proud parents) sends a clear message about the naptime expectations. We know it feels contrived to congratulate your child if he protested or struggled through an entire nap, but keep in mind that he is learning and you are praising him for his hard work.

+ *Shake off any difficulties, and don't give up.* Once the nap is over, try your best to leave it behind you. That'll be easy if it was a good nap, but if your baby struggled, moving on may be a bit more challenging. Still, just because one nap doesn't go smoothly doesn't mean the next one will be difficult. Forget about this one. That way, your head will be in the game for the next opportunity to sleep.

It's Ultimately Your Child's Choice to Nap

Many parents are surprised to hear that children don't have to sleep during a nap if they don't want to. They can sit in their cribs and talk, roll around, or play with their lovey. They can also cry to see if it'll work to pull you in and rescue them.

If you've followed our advice and started working on sleep at bedtime, you should have plenty of proof that your child is fully capable of putting herself to sleep. It may take some work, but try to remember that a baby will choose to cry if she thinks she's supposed to do that to get you back in her room. By following the nap schedule and giving her space to learn, you're showing her that naptime happens regardless of whether she wants to cry, play, or sleep. Once she catches on to this, she'll be much calmer in her crib, which will allow her to relax into sleep. As a bonus, she'll start to think of her crib as a safe place to practice new tricks (like discovering her feet, practicing standing up, or saying "mama") when she's not feeling tired.

What to Expect on the Way to Independent Sleep

Every child has a different journey on the road to independent sleep, but there are some general milestones to look for. Try not to think something is wrong if your child seems to be following a different time line. We're sharing these only to give you an idea of where you're headed and to show you where you'll likely see improvement along the way.

Days 2 and 3

For many children, the first night of sleep teaching is the most challenging because it's when they're introduced to the surprising new sleep plan. For other children, however, the second or third night is the most challenging. This is when they realize this new sleep situation is here to stay and they'd better put up some serious protesting so you know just how much they'd rather go back to the sleeping situation they had before. Even if your baby struggles more on nights 2 and 3 than she did on night 1, you should see progress in at least one or more areas during each twelve-hour night-time period.

Days 4 to 14

By this point, nighttime should be noticeably better. You baby may still struggle a bit at bedtime, may still be rousing early, or may be struggling at a certain point in the middle of the night, but if you are following the schedule, listening to your baby first, and being neutral if you do a crib check, then the cries will sound much softer and more "grunty." When parents are struggling during days 4 to 14, it is usually with the naps. Try to stick to the schedule we gave you because your baby will be going through so many changes over these two weeks. One day, naps are rough so nighttime is easy. Then naps are better because she is less overtired, but that makes nighttime harder because she isn't as tired at night.

Another common situation you may face is a sudden protest or random off-night. Until now, your child has been showing success with a string of great nights and then, seemingly out of nowhere, puts up a struggle one night. Many parents panic when this happens, but it is totally normal. It could be that your baby is better rested now after many nights of great sleep, so the nighttime sleep transitions feel different. A milestone could be popping up, or it could just be that he is checking to see if the new deal has relaxed at all. Whatever the reason, try to remain calm and do a crib check. If something is wrong (and it could be if the rousing is unusual), remedy the situation and give your child a chance to go back to sleep. If nothing is wrong, remember that your baby didn't suddenly forget how to fall asleep. Your job is to communicate your steadfast belief that he can sleep if nothing is wrong. If you can make it through this surprise protest and let your baby figure out how to put himself to sleep, the next day is likely to be perfect again. But if you are inconsistent and panic, one protest can lead to many more.

> If you need more motivation, look at your logs and remind yourself of how far your baby has come in such a short time.

Troubleshooting and Making Changes

If you're on your first day or two of sleep teaching and already consulting this section, it's probably a bit premature. We generally do not recommend you make any changes to your child's schedule until you've tried at least three days (but preferably two weeks) of sleep teaching.

Sometimes it's necessary to tweak your child's schedule during sleep teaching. If your gut is telling you that a different naptime is better for your child, trust it. But if you make any of the following modifications, stick with any of those changes for three days and nights so your baby has a chance to adapt. It's a bad idea to constantly move the target and make it impossible for your baby to meet your goal.

Nighttime Troubleshooting

Here are some things to consider if you see issues continuing at night after the first week. As long as you're paying close attention to these areas so you can rule them out, the answer is most likely that your baby's just adjusting on a slower time line—and that's normal.

Still Experiencing Multiple Nighttime Rousings? Check These:

- [ ] **Quality of feedings.** Sometimes babies who rouse a lot at night are uncomfortable because they are looking for more sustenance in their diet (say, an eight month old is ready for heartier foods). Make sure your baby is eating enough solids during the day. If he is under six months and trying to take more than thirty-two ounces of breast milk or formula during the day, you may want to ask your pediatrician if you can add some oatmeal (review Chapter Six on adding solids). If your baby is exclusively breast-fed, experiment by offering a bottle of expressed breast milk after feedings for a day and see if your baby wants more to eat. If your baby doesn't want the extra milk, you can rule out hunger as a reason for your baby's rousings.

- [ ] **Excessive crib checks.** After the first night or two, you should be getting more confident about whether your baby needs you. If you're still doing several crib checks at night and your child is still rousing frequently, your checks may be starting to work against you. Also, make sure you're staying completely neutral when you need to go in the room. If you're reacting at all to your baby, you may be rewarding the crying and encouraging more of it.

☐ **Late bedtime.** If your baby's bedtime is close to 8:00 P.M., you may want to consider moving to a 7:00 or 7:30 P.M. bedtime schedule. Sometimes when bedtimes are too late, babies get overly tired and their bodies produce cortisol, which can make it hard for them to settle properly into sleep cycles since cortisol gives bodies a boost of adrenaline.

Still Experiencing Early Morning Risings? Check These:

☐ **Quality of feedings.** Sometimes babies who rouse early are also looking for more sustenance during the daytime. See more information in "Still Experiencing Multiple Nighttime Rousings?"

☐ **Late bedtime.** It may seem counterintuitive, but sometimes an earlier bedtime can actually encourage another hour to an hour and a half of sleep in the morning.

☐ **Too much daytime sleep.** If your baby's bedtime is already around 7:00 P.M. and he is still having difficulty falling back to sleep in the early morning, it's possible he's getting too much daytime sleep. This can happen when babies are on the cusp of reaching an age where they're ready to drop a nap (for example, a six month old who's still taking three naps). If you aren't quite ready to make the switch to the next schedule, the key is to cut down a bit on the nap that is going to be phased out. For children on three naps, shortening the *third* nap by fifteen to thirty minutes usually works. For children on two naps, moving the *morning* nap thirty minutes later and dropping the bonus sleep (so the nap is only an hour) will do the trick.

☐ **Acceptance.** The schedules we include in this book are based on twelve hours of nighttime sleep because these are the schedules we find work best for our clients. But we also understand that babies and families aren't robots, and eleven hours of independent sleep at night is nothing to sneer at. Although our recommendation is always to start sleep teaching with the confidence that your child can be a twelve-hour sleeper, if this proves too challenging, simply consider adjusting to an eleven-hour nighttime schedule. Just remember that you'll probably need to make the naps slightly earlier or longer so you can add this missed hour of sleep into the daytime. Also sometimes when clients adjust the wake-up time to come earlier, the baby starts to view wake-up time as negotiable and rouses earlier and earlier. If this happens, set boundaries and follow a consistent wake-up time regardless of when your baby actually rouses for the day. Doing so will help keep her sleep on track in the long run.

The Double Diaper Recipe

Once your baby learns to go through the night without a feeding, whatever's waking your baby up is probably something external that you can help fix. Maybe she needs more food during the day, darker curtains, or a pain reliever for a virus or teething. Another common culprit is a chronically leaking diaper. If you don't fix it, it can disrupt your baby's sleep habits because there's too much interaction at night. If your baby is notorious for leaking through her diaper and standard overnight diapers aren't doing the trick, try our double diaper recipe:

1. Put your baby in one superabsorbent diaper. If you have a son, make sure his man part is pointing down.
2. Rip a little tear (about two inches) in the front of the diaper to compromise it, but not so much that it rips all the way through the diaper. This gives urine a pathway through the diaper instead of running over and up the top or along the sides.
3. Then put a nighttime pull-up-style diaper over the regular diaper. Make sure the pull-up is big enough to completely cover

the diaper on the top and through the thighs. The double diaper is now ready for action.

4. In the morning, remove the double diaper by reaching in and undoing the diaper tabs. Then pull everything off together by removing the pull-up down diaper (like pulling down underwear).

Daytime Troubleshooting

It's heartbreaking when babies struggle with naps. You can feel as if you're asking too much, especially since they seem so small and helpless. But have faith: when children are small, things are actually a little more straightforward than when they are older. Babies definitely need several intervals of daytime sleep each day!

Advice for Children on a Three-Nap Schedule

+   *Struggling with the last nap of the day.* It's usually not worth working to master the last nap of the day if your baby is having a hard time. This nap is usually phased out around six months of age, but if the other naps are challenging, it can become the final straw in terms of your own coping ability. If your baby is struggling, turn this nap into a stroller or car-seat nap. Since on-the-go naps aren't as restful, your baby may be overly tired by bedtime, but it will give him a little rest to be able to make it until bedtime.

+   *Rising early from a nap.* There's not a whole lot you can do if your child is rising early from the first or second nap other than have patience. Make sure you aren't getting your baby up earlier than the scheduled wake-up time; also, check that feedings are on schedule and satisfying. Make sure the room is very dark and the white noise is loud enough. However, don't forget that if your baby is struggling with the third nap, you can turn this one into a stroller or car-seat nap.

* *Not taking any naps.* It's rare, but it does happen: a young baby flat-out refuses any naps. If this is your situation and you're worried about your child being exhausted, here's your parachute as a last resort before quitting: make all of the naps stroller, car-seat, or swing naps and focus purely on the night sleep. This recommendation is only for the babies under six months of age. Continue to follow the scheduled times; just put your baby in a place where it's easier for him to fall asleep. Most likely, if your baby is used to being nursed to sleep, the stroller or car-seat nap is still going to teach him something about falling asleep on his own—in a different way that gives you a little more mental energy to focus on the nights. However, this will probably make your total teaching period longer than two weeks, so adjust your expectations accordingly.

* *An exhausted baby even though sleep is going well.* If your baby is napping and still seems totally exhausted, it's normal. He is not operating on adrenaline anymore so his body is adjusting and playing catch-up. Run through your schedule and make sure you're letting him take all the optional bonus naptime factored into his sleep schedule. If he's taking a good midday nap, you can try extending this nap from one hour with a thirty-minute bonus to ninety minutes with an hour bonus. As you make the midday nap longer, try to take time away from the third nap of the day. We know this next part is a bit complicated, but some clients have also been able to push the second nap later by half an hour and make it a two-hour nap with a thirty-minute bonus. Then they do a short catnap (optional) in the evening, about three hours before bedtime, for no more than twenty or thirty minutes (either in the crib or a stroller). If the nighttime sleep changes at all, make sure the optional catnap isn't too long or too late.

Advice for Children on a Two-Nap Schedule

+ *Difficulty falling asleep for first nap.* In the beginning of sleep teaching, your baby may fall asleep for the first nap relatively easily. But sometimes after the nighttime sleep gets better, children initially aren't tired enough to nap. Before deciding to drop the morning nap and switching to a one-nap schedule, try pushing the morning one fifteen minutes later. This is still a one-hour nap, but the bonus naptime is cut down to fifteen minutes. So if your nap is usually 9:00 to 10:00 A.M. with a thirty-minute bonus, it would change to 9:15 to 10:15 with a fifteen-minute bonus. If this helps but doesn't completely fix the problem, try pushing the nap another fifteen minutes later and dropping the bonus altogether. Another reason that your baby might have difficulty with the first nap is that she isn't completing the entire twelve to twelve and a half hours of sleep. If you've modified the wake-up time to be earlier than twelve hours, or you're waking your baby at twelve hours and not allowing her to sleep twelve and a half hours if she wants to, it's possible your baby is overly tired by the time this nap is occurring. Fixing the nighttime sleep so your baby is better rested may allow her to relax into this nap more easily.

+ *Difficulty falling asleep for second nap.* Your baby may not be tired enough to take the second nap, so try cutting back on the morning nap first (using the above suggestions). The afternoon nap will be a part of your child's life until he is three to four years old, so adjusting the morning nap is usually a better place to start. If you're happy with the first nap and don't want to change it, the second-best option is make the second nap a little later. Shortening this nap by pushing it later in fifteen-minute increments over a series of days may help you find the best time. If you choose this option, just be sure that you don't change the wake-up time so your baby will still have a full four hours of activity before bedtime.

+ *Not taking any naps.* If your baby's not on the cusp of switching to one nap and consistently refusing to sleep for both naps, our best advice (although hard to hear) is to stay the course. Be consistent; some babies learn on a slower timetable than others. As long as you are continuing to see progress in some part of your baby's sleep times (even if it's only nighttime progress), you can be sure that it's working. Just to be on the safe side, walk through your checklist. Make sure the nutrition is appropriate, check the anxiety level in the house, and make sure crib checks are used only for serious concerns and that you haven't skipped a step in the sleep environment. If you're doing all of the above and your baby isn't sick, take a step back and give your baby some space to learn.

Advice for Children on a One-Nap Schedule

+ *Difficulty falling asleep for nap.* Is your baby acting tired? Unless the nap is happening very early in the day, it's unlikely this issue is a scheduling one. Moving the nap a little later and cutting down on the overall time may seem like a good solution here, but it's not likely to fix the problem. Once babies are fifteen months or older, they have the strength to stay awake all day without taking a nap for weeks—sometimes even a month. Remind yourself that your child has a choice about how she spends her time in her crib. If she's on the right schedule and you're doing everything we taught you, she is mostly likely waiting to see if you'll change your mind about the nap. Remember that your baby is too young to go without one, so the only option is for her to eventually accept the nap. Be consistent; making what may seem like a small concession can build your baby's hope of being successful in resisting the nap.

+ *Rising early from nap.* If your baby is rising early from the nap, it's important to look at some other factors. What is the child's behavior like at night? Is he getting a solid twelve hours of sleep? If he's completely fine in the evening and sleeping soundly for the full twelve hours, then it's possible to cut off the nap early (but make sure the nap is a minimum of one hour). Stick with it over a period of time. That way, you can see if the shorter nap is or isn't affecting your child. If your baby starts having multiple rousings at night and acting overly tired and cranky in the evening, these are signs he may need more of a nap, so keep working on it.

Additional Troubleshooting

If you make schedule changes and still don't see some improvement after a few days, something else may be going on. Review the sections that follow, and determine if any of these other sleep inhibitors could be hindering your child's progress.

Sickness

If you've gone through your checklist and your baby is still having hours of wakefulness at night or struggling for naps, it may be that she's physically uncomfortable due to unmanaged reflux or illness. The best way to rule out illness is to take your child to the doctor. If you just started training and your baby has a temperature above 100 degrees Fahrenheit, it's probably best not to push the training until the fever drops. Having a fever doesn't mean a child can't fall asleep on her own; however, if you just started training, it's going to be hard to give her the mental space she needs to learn. We want to set everyone up for success, not more frustration. If your baby is sick and you've been training for a week or so and she's now falling asleep at night with no problem, you can choose to allow her to fall asleep on her own and continue to follow the bones of the schedule— offering more sleep or less as necessary. That way, she can continue to take advantage of her new great sleep, and you can tighten things back up when she's better.

Milestones

When children start to sleep through the night, they can start to achieve important milestones—seemingly in a burst. We'll discuss this more in the next chapter, but keep in mind these milestones may be coupled with sleep disruptions. Once the milestone transition is over, your baby will go back to sleeping well. There's not anything you can do, aside from helping her to work on this milestone during the waking hours. So if your baby learns to roll over on day 5 of sleep teaching, it's okay to keep going. Use your one-time pass rule and give her lots of time to practice her new skill throughout the day.

Child Care Providers

Sometimes nannies and babysitters are inconsistent when parents are not around. If you have a baby who was taking good naps and going down easily at night and then somewhat suddenly starts having trouble, make sure all of your caregivers are following the same playbook.

Sweet Dreams!

Even parents and caregivers with the best intentions can make mistakes. If you make a mistake in your plan or just simply cave in one night, give yourself a break. Maybe you instinctively picked up your child during a crib check. Perhaps your babysitter forgot to turn on the white noise machine for a nap. We're all human. Sure, it may have made things a little more difficult for your child, but it was an honest mistake, so forgive yourself or your caregiver. Adults deserve a one-time pass too. However, if it happens more often than not, it may be time to check commitment levels—your own and your child care provider's. Staying committed is the key to keeping things going and ensuring your child's long-term success as a great sleeper.

From Stubborn and Sensitive Sleeper to World Traveler

YAEL AND KEN N., PARENTS OF CRUZ

You helped us put sleep training in perspective. Cruz, our son, was a very stubborn and strong-willed boy, and it took a long time for the training to work. He was resistant to all the newly set boundaries and cried a lot, and it took a solid two weeks of crying for forty-five minutes to an hour for him to get to sleep each time he went to bed.

192

It was so hard for me, and I cried every night, but you kept telling me it would be worth it and to just keep on believing in him and our new routine. Still, we knew that in order for us to have a new life, we needed to sleep-teach our son. If we wanted to go back to hours of rocking him to sleep and being awake at four to six points in the night, then we could give up, but we knew it wasn't worth it. So we stuck with it, and you were right: it changed our lives! Not only did we benefit from Cruz sleeping, but so did he. He was always a cheerful baby, but once he started sleeping, he was the happiest baby anyone had ever seen. It was as if the sleep allowed Cruz to show his true personality and let his giggles and laughs come through now that he could sleep better.

What helped us the most? The schedule helped in every way. I loved how straightforward and clear it was, how simple it made our lives. The nurturing list for the spouses to create was also a wonderful idea—and it's something we still talk about when things get stressful.

Sure, there are days when he doesn't sleep as well as he should, but in general, he's become an amazing sleeper. In the first twelve months of his sleep, he traveled to the West Coast seven times and was on more than thirty airline trips. Besides our international travel to Asia (admittedly a disaster), not one single trip had a sleepless night.

CHAPTER 12

Keeping It Going

Now that your baby is sleeping better, it's time to let you in on a little secret: if you want a good sleeper for years to come, you'll never fully graduate from working on sleep.

Although your child's sleep schedule won't change much over the next few years, sleep issues creep up when you least expect them. Our own kids have sleep hiccups from time to time because despite our doing everything (or most things) right, children change and test limits. This is part of growing up, which you most certainly want them to do. It just means that we need to adapt to keep up.

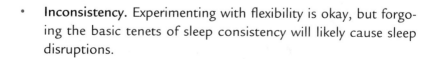

Keys to Zzzs

Here are some of the most common sleep challenges you may face in the months or years to come:

- **Inconsistency.** Experimenting with flexibility is okay, but forgoing the basic tenets of sleep consistency will likely cause sleep disruptions.

- **Sickness and teething.** When your baby's not feeling well, it's probably going to interfere with sleep teaching.
- **Travel.** Being in unfamiliar surroundings can cause your baby to feel out of sorts and not as relaxed about sleeping.
- **Daylight Saving Time changes.** Time changes can have an effect on anyone's circadian clock—and this can be true for babies too.
- **Major milestones.** Reaching a new level of growth, like potty training or dropping naps, can significantly interfere with sleep patterns.
- **Moving to a toddler bed.** You may find it challenging to keep your toddler in his new bed.
- **Arrival of a sibling.** New babies can make sleep a bit more challenging for toddlers.

~~~~~~

When you hit bumps in the road, simply brush up on the tools you used to teach your child to sleep initially and swiftly guide her back to a good sleep place.

"The basics of your philosophy hold true as William ages. I've used your same principles for sleep teaching when my son has experienced other challenges as he's gotten older—post-illness waking, transition to the big boy bed, or the recent arrival of bad dreams. The same concept of giving loving reassurance followed by confident putting-back-to-bed has allowed us to maintain good sleep patterns."
—MOLLY AND CHAD L., PARENTS OF WILLIAM

Inconsistency

Inconsistency is at the root of most sleep issues that will pop up in your child's life. The more consistent you are about your child's sleep, the harder it is for your child to be confused about what she should be doing. Imagine your child's sleep habits are like a bank account. Every day you are consistent is like making a regular deposit. Inconsistency is like going on a shopping spree. Maybe it's okay occasionally, but a shopping spree too often can result in a lot of financial discomfort. We understand that sometimes you don't have a choice; maybe your baby has a doctor appointment during a naptime, gets a stomach virus, or you have a huge travel day. It's good to remember that given these inevitable inconsistencies, the more consistent you can be on a regular basis when life is running normally, the better off you and your baby will be.

If you get off track, reestablish your sleep parameters. Things will never be as hard as they were at the start of sleep teaching. Once your baby learns to put himself to sleep, he has this skill for life.

Sometimes past clients need additional support in recovering from some inconsistencies. In nearly every case, we help them to do the following:

- Tighten up on a sleep schedule and follow the nap rules completely.
- Do brief, neutral crib checks.
- Check your child's behavior during the day to make sure he isn't getting mixed messages (for example, that rule breaking is acceptable during daytime).

Sickness and Teething

It's not a good idea to start the sleep teaching process or be rigid in adhering to your sleep rules when your baby is sick. However, after sleep teaching, your child has learned how to be an independent sleeper, so our recommendations change a bit. Just because your baby is sick doesn't mean she has forgotten how to put herself to sleep. In fact, when babies are sick, they need more sleep than usual.

So do you just ignore your baby's midnight cries when he is sick? Of course not! If your baby is sick and you suspect that he needs you, then you should go in and check on him. If he needs your help, by all means, help him. If he needs to be cleaned up, clean him up. If he has a temperature, give him something for it or help cool him down and wait for the fever to drop. Just try not to fall back on your old sleeping habits. It will be tempting in the moment. But going back to the thing your child once "needed" from you to fall asleep (say, sleeping with you) can make it much harder for your child in the long run. If you go back to the old routine, the transition can be really hard when it's time to get back to normal again.

Also keep in mind there are varying levels of sickness. You might notice your daughter has a cough or is a little fussy due to teething. If she isn't running a fever and she isn't congested, you may choose to give her some over-the-counter medicine (according to your doctor's advice, of course) for teething pain. But then the best thing you can do is help her know that she needs to go back to bed. The best way to communicate that is to check on her and be confident sleep will help her feel better.

Chances are pretty good that your baby's going to have the sniffles at regular intervals for the first several years of life. He's also going to experience teething for many years. These are not always reasons to undo all the work that he has done in sleep learning. If your child can learn to how to sleep through some of these times, it'll help avoid a lot of unnecessary crying when you start getting back to a good place again.

Mostly, relax and expect things to be a little off when kids aren't feeling quite right. You can let your baby sleep a little longer if she needs the extra sleep. Be sensitive to wake-up times and adjust earlier or later as necessary. And certainly be highly responsive to make sure that she's okay. Do anything you need to do in the night (a steam shower, a little TV, medicine, cuddling on the couch) to make her feel comfortable, but when it's time to sleep, try to put her in the crib awake. At first, you'll be nervous, but you'll see that she is actually quite comfortable going to sleep on her own if you're calm. If it's not happening, don't worry. You can get back to normal once your child is healthy again.

"It's okay to give acetaminophen or ibuprofen fifteen to twenty minutes before bedtime if your child is uncomfortable from teething. Use your baby's weight to determine proper dosage, and do not use ibuprofen for infants less than six months of age."

—DR. AMY DEMATTIA, PEDIATRICIAN

Travel

One thing our clients like the most about our approach to sleep is that it helps them enjoy their vacations and trips away from home. Once your child is a consistent sleeper, it's much easier to draw on those skills in a new sleeping space. It's all about recreating her perfect sleeping space and trying to keep her on her schedule.

Here are some basics for traveling.

Preparing Hosts

It's a good idea to set expectations about your sleep plan before you arrive at your destination, so the people you are visiting—say, grandparents—can manage their expectations about certain limitations you will have once you arrive. Send the schedule ahead of time and emphasize how well it's working at home. You might even want to circle the naps that you are willing to do on the run so that Grandma can schedule her annual apple picking outing accordingly. Before the first nap or night, talk your hosts through crying and what it means. Remind them that you can hear the baby and you're not ignoring him. Tell them that you aren't making the baby cry; you're giving him a chance to fall asleep.

Getting to Your Destination

It's also a good idea to plan your departures and arrivals as carefully as you can so you can keep your baby on his schedule. Here are some general guidelines for smoother travels:

+ *Road trips.* Try to schedule shorter car trips (under three hours) during your baby's naptime so he has time to play when you get to your destination. If possible, plan to leave for longer trips (over three hours) around bedtime; that way, you don't disturb your first period of deep sleep. Sometimes parents who accidentally wake their baby up in the middle of this cycle can unintentionally cause her to have a night terror—something to avoid on vacation.

+ *Airplane travel.* The rule of thumb is to plan to leave at a time that doesn't require your baby to wake up for the day too early. Even one early rising can lead to more early risings, and most people don't want to wake up before the sun rises every day, especially while on vacation. It's generally better to put your baby in her crib past her bedtime than have to wake her up early to get on the road.

+ *Getting settled in.* When you arrive at your destination, don't forsake your normal bedtime routine, even if it's late. If your child falls asleep in the car, wake him up when you arrive, do part of the together time routine (like show your baby where he will sleep and read one short book), and put him in his crib to sleep. If you arrive in the daytime, your nap schedule is likely to be a bit off. Just try to make sure the wake-up from the last nap of the day is three to four hours before bedtime. Then your baby will bounce right back on schedule. If your baby goes down at night later than her usual bedtime, simply start the next day by rousing her around her normal wake-up time. You may have a grumpy baby for a day, but she will adjust.

Here are a few tips for making your baby's sleeping space while you are away from home feel familiar:

- Try to spend some time before bedtime getting acquainted in the place your child will be sleeping. Bring a few special toys from home so your child can recognize this as his space.
- Show your baby his lovey, and let him see you put it in his crib.
- Bring the white noise machine from home, plug it in, and show your baby that you brought his noise.
- Use black garbage bags to serve as blackout curtains if your destination doesn't have them.

"We were skeptical about traveling after sleep training. By keeping the environment and routine the same, she did great! We travel with one white noise machine and have purchased another for our second child."
—KRISTEN AND BRIAN M., PARENTS OF SOPHIE

If your baby sleeps in a crib, try to arrange to have a full-size crib wherever you're visiting. If this isn't possible, a portable crib will be just fine. If your stay is a long one or there's a place you visit often, you can get a play yard mattress that fits snuggly inside the portable crib.

Schedules on Vacation

If you've recently wrapped up sleep teaching, you're probably ready to leave the house and take your wonderful sleeper on the road. If possible, try to make those first few trips as seamless and easy as possible. Make sure your baby has his own space, endeavor to stick to the sleep schedule as much as possible, and continue to be consistent with how you respond to him at night.

In terms of daytime schedule, if you're on a vacation, you're likely to have planned some fun activities. Vacations are special and meant for enjoying, so you don't need to stick to a strict schedule. A few stroller or car seat naps are okay; just try not to do too many in a row if possible. And if you need to choose between which naps to skip, opt for doing the second or third one on the road. Preserving the quality of the first nap will help set a good foundation for the day.

If your child has been a solid sleeper for a while, you can be a little more lenient if she wakes in the night or rises much too early in the morning while you are on vacation. Start by giving her a few minutes to fall back asleep. If she doesn't appear to be settling down, do a quick crib check to make sure everything is okay. If things still don't settle down, you can give her a little break. Keep the lights low but it's okay to get your baby up, sing a song, or walk around to show her where you are. Once your child has calmed down and she sees that everyone else is asleep so it is totally boring, then it is time to sleep. Make sure that whatever you do, you put her in her crib awake. Also resist the temptation to bring her into bed with you or nurse or rock to sleep if that was something your baby used to do before you fixed sleep. Vacation is not the time for sleep teaching, but if you can avoid falling back on bad habits, you won't undo all the strides you have made to this point. The next night will probably be perfect, and if it's not, you can tighten things back up when you return home.

Changing Time Zones

When you cross only one time zone, you may decide that adjusting the schedule isn't necessary. When you cross multiple time zones, however, it's a good idea to have a plan for helping your child adjust. In general, children are more sensitive to light than adults are, so use this to defeat jet lag. Get outside and into fresh air. Also, use meals to help your child's body adjust to the new time. As soon as possible, adopt the new time and give your child three daily meals accordingly.

If you take an overnight flight, get ready for anything but hope for the best. Chances are your child will get a long stretch of sleep during the flight. However, he will still be tired on arrival; no one ever gets off a plane feeling great, and babies are no exception. Adjust your clock, and try not to think about what time it is at home. Give your baby a day to adjust by letting him take some extra-long naps, but try to keep him up for the last three or so hours before his bedtime (at the new destination time). This will help end the day at the "right" time and set the stage for the following day. On day 2, assume your child will have mostly adjusted, and try to reimplement your normal sleep schedule.

If you travel late into the night and arrive at your destination with an awake (and excited) baby at 1:00 A.M., try your best to get your child back down to sleep once you are inside. If she wants to sleep late in the morning, let her catch up on sleep. The next day, try to expose your baby to sunlight, and don't let her take more than one or two two-hour naps (waking up within three to four hours of bedtime). Put your baby in her crib as close as possible to the regular bedtime and wake her at the normal time. If she goes down earlier than usual for bedtime, she may wake up earlier. If that happens, try to stretch the naps to happen later and later until your baby can go to bed as close to the normal bedtime as possible.

If you arrive at your destination midday, try to help your child go to bed close to her normal bedtime at the new destination time. This may be easy or difficult depending on how the first part of the day went and the number of time zones crossed. The day after you arrive, rouse your baby at her normal wake-up time. Expose her to sunlight, continue to follow the new time, and try to stick to her normal eating and sleeping schedule. There may be some over- or under-tiredness, but it should start to smooth out on day 3.

Expect that once you return home, your baby will be overtired and a bit out of sync. Consistency with your response, schedule, and listening skills will help you and your baby recover from the trip as soon as possible.

Daylight Saving Time

Parents of sensitive sleepers often dread Daylight Saving Time. We recommend starting the time transition on the Saturday of a time change during naptime and bedtime:

+ *Spring:* If your child has two to three naps during the day, move the naps up in fifteen-minute increments. If your child has one nap a day, move it up by thirty minutes and push his bedtime up another thirty minutes as well.
+ *Fall:* If your child has two to three naps during the day, move them back in fifteen-minute increments. If your child has one nap a day, move it back by thirty minutes and push his bedtime back by another thirty minutes as well.

Getting a head start on the time adjustment will give you the benefit of an extra day of fine-tuning before Monday rolls around (and work and school schedules pick up again).

Try your best to get your child ready for these modified sleep times by getting plenty of fresh air. If possible, introduce some novel activities to help tire your child out a bit more than usual. Also, stick to your usual presleep routine if you have one. By Sunday morning, after the clocks have been adjusted overnight, wake your child up at her normal time and put her down at her normal naptimes. This may be a challenge the first day or so, since it'll feel an hour early or late to her little body.

Continue to get outside and have even more active play planned for your family on Sunday. On Sunday evening, try your best to help your child be in his pajamas and ready for bed at his normal bedtime, according to the new time. Again, stick to your usual bedtime routine as if nothing has changed.

+ *Spring:* If your child is not showing signs of being tired, it's okay to make bedtime fifteen to thirty minutes later (according to the new clock) and continue to refine the schedule the next day. Also, it will be much lighter outside at bedtime than your child was accustomed to. You may need to add blackout shades again if you took them down during the winter.

+ *Fall:* If your child is exhausted, it's okay to put her in her crib fifteen to thirty minutes early (according to the new clock) and continue to refine the schedule the next day.

All children are different. Some make the jump in time change seamlessly, and others take a few days to fully adjust. Just be patient and it will all "spring" or "fall back" into place.

Milestones

Milestones are amazing times of growth for your child. The downside is they can cause some temporary frustration, which can interfere with sleep temporarily. For example, your child may be practicing standing up and have difficulty falling back to sleep throughout the night because she is so excited about her new skill. How you respond to your child when she learns a new behavior is important. If you notice your child is on the cusp of a certain behavior, it's always good to practice during the day and mentally prepare yourself to be calm and nonreactive at night.

Here are some milestones to keep an eye out for and how to help ease the transition:

+ *Rolling over:* At night when your child rolls over and is upset, go in and do the one-time pass. Do not roll her back onto her front. Instead, show her she's okay on her stomach by turning her head very gently to the side. The reason we don't suggest rolling your baby onto her back is that she is going to roll right back over again. The more you roll her back, the more she wants to do it because it can quickly become a game. Since you aren't going to get her to stop rolling, helping her learn to be comfortable in this new position from the beginning is key. Help her strengthen her core during the day by doing lots of tummy time and practicing rolling over on a play mat. Also, once your baby starts rolling over, it's time to lower the crib.

+ *Sitting and standing up:* Some babies sit up for the first time in their crib and get stuck. At night, do a one-time pass and show him how to lie down. If your baby is sitting, guide his shoulders down to the mattress. If standing, take his hands from the crib rail and hold them as you guide him to a seated position or he lies down. Be careful not to pick your baby up or you could communicate that he needs to be elevated to get out of that position. Practice helping him lie down from a sitting or standing position during the day by putting a favorite toy just slightly out of reach so he has to lean or sit down to get it. The more practice during the day, the more prepared he will be and the more confident you will feel once he goes to bed.

+ *Language bursts:* Language bursts may be accompanied with extra crying and sleep protests. A big one usually happens around the first birthday and a few others happen throughout the second year. Run through your checklist if your child is struggling with sleep. Healthy baby? Right sleep schedule? Right food? Good exercise? Consistency from parents? It is going to feel confusing when your perfect sleeper has a hiccup, but try your hardest not to overrespond or change the schedule too early because your baby will resume her old habits once she's through processing her new communication skills.

Moving to a Toddler Bed

Sleeping in a toddler bed is much different from sleeping in a crib, emotionally speaking. While some children are capable of switching earlier, it's best to wait as long as possible before phasing out the crib, ideally about the time your child is around three years old.

When toddlers are old enough and are sleeping consistently well enough in a crib, then it is a great time to reward them with a "big boy" or "big girl" bed. The first step is to pay close attention to his behavior during the day. For instance, if you've gotten into certain patterns with your child (maybe she constantly gets out of her booster during mealtimes or throws tantrums when you say no until you give in), it is likely that this behavior will spill over into the nighttime once there are no longer any boundaries around her sleeping space. Your best strategy is to fix a few of these behavioral issues before you switch to the toddler bed. Give a warning with an immediate consequence ("If you throw that toy one more time, I will take it away."). You must follow through! A few days of paying close attention to the little things can make a big difference when you introduce the toddler bed, because your child will have a fresh understanding that you mean what you say. Working on this behavior is no fun, but it doesn't have to be a cloud over this huge childhood transition.

When it *is* time for the toddler bed, get excited about the change. Involve your child by letting him help choose his favorite superhero sheets and allowing him to "help" you convert the crib into a toddler bed. You can also do some dramatic play with animals showing a baby sleeping in a bed with parents waking him up. Before bedtime on the first night, sit down in a quiet place and explain that even though the bed is different, the deal is the same: he should stay in his bed if he wakes up and you will wake him up in the morning as usual. If your child comes out of his room at night now that he has the ability to leave his bed, be calm, with no sudden jerks or facial reactions. Simply take his hand and lead him back to bed. The first time he gets out, you can say, "It is time to sleep. We will come and get you when it is time to wake up." It may take a few trips (or 250 trips), but if you've been consistent about your sleep boundaries when your baby was in a crib, he may not get up at all. Waiting until your child already has good sleeping habits and is emotionally ready to be in a bed (around three years) will help make the transition much easier.

Arrival of a Sibling

Welcoming a new brother or sister into the family is an exciting moment in any child's life. However, with the highs can come some lows. Anticipation and joy are usually coupled with some amount of jealousy and confusion. When it comes to sleep, it's helpful to make major changes, such as giving up a bottle or pacifier, several months before the new baby arrives. If you plan to use your older child's crib for the baby, move her to her toddler bed well in advance of the birth (assuming she's old enough and emotionally ready). If possible, purchase new bedding for the crib so your child doesn't feel nostalgic for her old sleeping quarters.

It's also helpful to start modifying your child's bedtime routine before the new baby arrives. As much as you love bedtime, you'll have less one-on-one time to go around the first few months with a newborn. Give your child a chance to adjust to a new way of winding down at the end of the day. Maybe that means streamlining her bedtime ritual a bit. Maybe it means letting Dad do more of the bedtime duties. Just try not to act sad about the changes yourself (even if you are).

Dropping Naps

You'll know your child is ready to drop a nap when she begins resisting it day after day for at least one straight week. That way, you can eliminate sickness or another life transition as the reason. Be careful not to jump the gun; a few days of nap resistance isn't a clear indication it's time to change her nap schedule. Teething, travel, milestones, sickness, and life transitions all make naps harder at times.

But if your child starts resisting naps or starts rousing more than an hour earlier each morning for at least one full week (an indicator that she is getting too much naptime), it's time to consider a transition to a new nap schedule. See Chapter Five for schedule suggestions by age. If your child falls within the age range of a different schedule, then your can be confident that it's time to drop or shorten a nap. What works best for most children is to make the decision to drop the nap and not go back.

In the beginning, try to fill your day with extra fun in the form of energizing activities. Avoid putting her in a car seat or stroller when she's looking especially sleepy. If children fall asleep in the late morning, even just for ten to fifteen minutes, many won't be able to take a solid afternoon nap, which they do need if they move to a one-nap schedule.

If your baby's struggling to make it to naptime, you may want to move the nap earlier by fifteen to thirty minutes. You can do the same with bedtime if your child is falling asleep during dinner. Don't be discouraged if your child struggles; keep reminding yourself to believe in his ability to sleep and that crying is a choice once you know he can fall asleep on his own.

Dropping a nap can be a slow process for some children, but most are able to fully adjust in a few weeks.

Potty Training

Potty training is a major developmental milestone, usually occurring between the ages of two and three years. Expect some temporary life disturbances, including in the sleep department.

It's best to focus initially only on daytime potty training. Even if you go without diapers while your child is awake, we recommend you continue to put her in a diaper at both naptime and nighttime in the beginning. Once her diaper has been dry for two consecutive weeks during naps, she may be ready to graduate to twelve-hour diaper-free days. However, don't rush diaper-free nights. Nighttime potty training can take quite some time for children to completely master—months or even years.

Parting Thoughts About Flexibility and Rules

Once your baby is sleeping wonderfully, it's okay to be flexible and experiment. You can bend the rules. In fact, do bend the rules. The results may surprise you. You'll learn your child is pretty flexible or really isn't. Either way, it's good information.

Some of you may also decide to skip naptime one day for a lunch out, only to discover that lunch with your friend and fussy baby who just wants to be home sleeping in her crib isn't quite the lovely outing you imagined it to be.

Another probable scenario? You and your baby will end up at a friend's house one day, play too long, and all of a sudden, it's naptime. She offers to have him nap there, but you don't have her lovey and sound machine. You decide to proceed with the nap anyway, and your baby sleeps with no problem! How wonderful would that be?

Other parents may find that their babies aren't sensitive to light after all or that saying goodnight doesn't have to always be so quick.

It's all a learning process, but if any decisions you make end up causing your baby significant stress and frustration, you might want to consider not repeating it.

Personally, we're not slaves to the sleep schedule day in and day out. You may see us at a birthday party with a baby sleeping in the stroller. Or you may hear us talk about our child skipping a nap to go to a 1:00 P.M. Minor League baseball game. It's really okay to do these things as long as it's the exception and not the norm.

Parenting isn't about always being perfect. Going against your own rules doesn't always have negative consequences. Just make sure you're doing it because you want the change and not because your child is resisting something. Actually, discovering those areas of flexibility is exciting.

Sweet Dreams!

The advice contained in this book comes from a place of compassion for the families who are suffering with sleep challenges and want to make a positive, thoughtful change. For those of you who can rally for just a little bit of time to teach your child to sleep, we are certain of all the rewards that lie ahead for you and your family. And once things calm down, you will realize that you aren't "working" on sleep anymore. Then you can let it fall gently into the background of your day as the other new wonderful areas of growth take center stage.

It's never too late to teach your child to love sleep. So let's focus on it for a few weeks, with the idea that the rewards are *always* well worth the work!

We wish you the best of luck on your sleep journey!

Frequently Asked Questions

Newborn and Baby

Q: My two week old will sleep only if he's in our arms.

A: You shouldn't worry too much about your baby's independent sleep skills until he or she is about four months old. So if your newborn needs to be held or he will cry hysterically from 4:00 P.M. to 9:00 P.M., hold away. Just make sure you aren't so exhausted that you are inadvertently falling asleep while holding him. As much as you love your baby, if you're in a deep sleep while holding your baby, it's hard to be safe. Accidents happen all the time to loving parents, so do your best to safeguard against them.

Q: My baby is up all night and asleep all day. When do they grow out of this?

A: Babies do not produce melatonin the first six weeks or so of life. This is why day and night confusion is very normal among newborns, and there's not a whole lot you can do to change it. After six weeks of age, however, you can start to communicate that daytime is for fun and nighttime is for sleep. First, take your baby out of the house for at least an hour each day. New experiences and fresh air are stimulating. Sunlight also helps reset babies' sleep clocks. Second, make sure nighttime is extremely boring for your child. That means only basic interaction at times they should be sleeping. Even whispering to your baby can be an invitation to play.

Q: Is cosleeping safe?

A: The American Academy of Pediatrics recommends parents not sleep with infants in an adult bed, stating that the practice puts babies at risk of suffocation and strangulation. If you want your baby very close at night, cosleeper bassinets (bassinets that attach safely to the side of an adult bed) are an option for families interested in cosleeping during the first few months. We know that many people do decide to cosleep on a permanent basis. If you choose to share your bed with your baby, make sure to follow these safety precautions:

+ Always place your baby on her back.
+ Make sure your bed's headboard and footboard don't have openings or cutouts that could trap your baby's head.
+ Don't place a baby to sleep in an adult bed alone.
+ Don't use pillows, comforters, quilts, and other soft or plush items on the bed.
+ Don't drink alcohol or use medications or drugs that may keep you from waking and may cause you to roll over and accidentally harm your baby.

Q: How do I know when to stop swaddling?

A: Keeping a child swaddled for too long can start to be uncomfortable and may affect physical development. The optimal time to stop swaddling is between two and four months. At this point the Moro reflex (newborns' instinctive startle) has started to wane. When parents stop swaddling their children, they're often astonished to see how much they travel around their crib while they sleep. They move and flop from one end to the other several times a night. Babies may look peaceful when they sleep, but don't be fooled: they're actually doing important exercise while they slumber. A swaddled baby doesn't have a chance to refine these skills at night.

Q: When should I move my baby from a bassinet to a crib? From a crib to a bed?

A: There's no perfect time to move your child to a crib for sleep. Some children sleep exclusively in their crib from the start, and that's just fine. However, many parents keep their children in a bassinet or cosleeper at night because it makes nighttime feedings easier to manage. Most children start to grow out of bassinets around three to four months of age, so that is often a natural transition point for many families. When you're ready to make the move, try acclimating your baby to the crib first. Try having him nap once or twice a day there before you make it his full-time sleeping space. The best age for moving to a bed is around three years of age. Before that, children are very impulse driven and will have a hard time staying in their room if they are prone to problematic night wakings.

Q: Why doesn't my two-month-old baby sleep more than twenty minutes at a time?

A: If your baby is under eight to ten weeks and still cat napping all the time, don't worry. Short bursts of sleep at irregular intervals are normal at this age. Sleep will start to consolidate soon. After two months, you should aim for naps to be between forty-five and ninety minutes. If your little one is sleeping less than that, we have two recommendations. First, space naps an hour and a half to two hours apart to avoid letting your baby get overly tired and make the act of falling and staying asleep even more of a challenge. Second, make sure the nursery is sleep friendly: dark, between sixty-eight and seventy-two degrees, distraction free, and equipped with some white noise.

Q: Will a baby grow out of sleep issues?

A: Much like eating well, sleeping well is a skill that people hone and practice over a lifetime. We can't tell you how many people jokingly ask when we are going to start working with adults. The truth is, 40 percent of babies who have problematic night wakings at eight months of age still have sleep issues at four years of age. Those aren't great odds. Even if your child may outgrow poor sleep habits later, we think giving your baby the opportunity to be the best that she can be from the beginning is a true gift.

Q: At what age is it okay to start a schedule?

A: If you like schedules and thrive on having order to your day, you can start a loose schedule after eight weeks of age. (See our suggested schedule for two to four month olds in Chapter Five.) Just remember that many babies under four months still need a feeding or two at night. If your baby needs a feeding, feed him when he rouses and then try to put him back down as soon as he is finished. Also, if you do start a schedule early, try to have realistic expectations. Your child may not be able to conform to your ideal schedule every day, especially when you introduce it. However, by four months of age, children have more mature sleep cycles and are big enough to consume enough calories during the daytime, so they can follow a regular eating and feeding schedule.

Q: I don't think I can wait until my baby is four months old to get sleep. How can I cope?

A: There are some parents who are desperate for sleep after just a few weeks home with a newborn. There's not much you can do to teach your baby sleeping skills this early, but you can help yourself. Perhaps you can hire a night nurse or rely on family members to pull an occasional night shift. If you feel depressed or if your baby is starting to lose weight because she's so tired, make an appointment with your respective doctors before working on sleep teaching. Sleep teaching before sixteen weeks of age is frequently an uphill battle, so we don't usually recommend it. In terms of dealing with sleep deprivation, try to sleep whenever your baby does. We know it's hard to do that with everything else in your life you need to attend to, but it's very important for you to rest. This is easier said than done if you're relying on caffeine (we hazily recall hourly coffee breaks from 6:00 A.M. to 3:00 P.M. with our first kids), so our advice is to do everything you can to protect the first three hours of your nighttime sleep. This is when you're in your deepest, most restorative sleep. If you can find a few nights a week for uninterrupted deep sleep, your days will be much more enjoyable. Because sleep deprivation is related to postpartum depression and feelings of despair, avoiding a buildup of serious sleep loss is important.

Q: Our baby used to go to sleep easily, but now he wakes every hour or two, sometimes to be fed and sometimes to just be held.

A: This is very common, especially in children who are three to four months old. Your child is most likely experiencing a wakeful period. This period is associated with sleep regression because it's when children become much more aware of their surroundings and their connection to others. Increased curiosity and attachment to parents can cause sleep challenges to start cropping up, especially at bedtime. One way you can help your child though this period is by practicing short bursts of separation during the day (making sure the child is safe when you do). This shows babies that parents leave but always come back. It's also helpful to remember that development is not linear when it comes to babies and children. It looks more like a stock market chart than a straight line up a hill. They can have several great days or months of progress and then stumble a little. This is totally normal. It's our job as parents to maintain awareness of all the outside factors, like consistent response, consistent environment, and consistent schedule; remain supportive; and make sure the baby is not in pain or sick. By sticking to what you can control during the times that seem out of control, you'll help these periods be less disruptive. And when it's over, your baby will go back to sleeping like an angel.

Q: Should I ever wake a sleeping baby?

A: Yes! Particularly if it's the last nap of the day and bedtime is only a few hours away. A child who takes a four-hour nap in the afternoon most likely will have a hard time falling asleep at bedtime. Our sleep schedules provide you some flexibility in allowing your child to get some extra sleep if she needs it, but not too much that it starts to disrupt her nighttime schedule.

Q: Wouldn't it be best to use my sleep logs to find the bedtime that mirrors when my baby is the most tired? I don't want to mess with her naturally established sleep rhythms.

A: Bedtime is something parents should choose. If your life has felt a bit helter-skelter lately, we're guessing it feels liberating to be in control of something. Pick a bedtime between 6:00 and 8:00 P.M., and try to stick to it for the long term. Don't worry about your baby's current sleep patterns. If your baby goes to bed at midnight, it's okay to jump to this earlier bedtime (say, 7:30 P.M.) in one day. Our sleep teaching plan will help you time your day so your baby is ready for bed at the time *you* choose.

Toddler

Q: My twenty month old recently started climbing out of his crib, so we moved him into a toddler bed. Now I can't stop him from crawling into bed with us in the middle of the night. What can I do to stop this when I'm sleep teaching?

A: This dilemma is one of the reasons we recommend that parents keep their children in a crib until they are around three years old. Toddlers are impulse driven and not generally emotionally mature enough until they are three to understand that even though there are no sides on the bed, they are not supposed to get out of bed. If your child has already moved to a toddler bed, you have three options:

1. On the day of teaching, remove the toddler bed, and put the crib back in the room. Place some pillows on the floor around the crib to soften any accidental falls, and if he climbs out in the night, quietly put him back. It may take many, many rounds of putting him back in, but eventually he will stay.

2. Move the crib back into the room and use a crib tent to keep him from getting out. The downside to introducing a crib tent is that it can be difficult to travel with a child who is dependent on a crib tent to stay in a crib. More important, a crib tent does not actually teach your child to stay put. Some parents put a crib tent on initially to keep their baby safe until they are ready to teach their child to stay in the crib. Once you are prepared, remove the crib tent at bedtime and follow the steps in option 1.

3. Keep him in his toddler bed and live with the status quo until he is close to three. Then work on teaching him to stay in his room until morning. This isn't our recommendation because most young children do not feel comfortable in a toddler bed. Also, it isn't safe to have a toddler walking around the house when everyone else is asleep.

Q: We did sleep teaching at four months, and it worked well. Now that our daughter is a year old, she cries and cries as if something is wrong.

A: If your normally solid sleeper falls off the track, it's a good idea to go back to basics. Could she be ill (maybe she has an ear infection)? Did you just return from a vacation where she may have been off schedule? Is she going through a major milestone such as learning how to walk or a language burst? It's normal to have bumps in the road, and when that happens, just tighten up on your schedule and make sure her bedtime is as simple as possible. That way, you can remind her that the sleeping parameters you once established still apply—even though she feels different. Eventually she'll feel comforted by having boundaries around sleep, and the protesting will fade.

Q: What do I do if my child is head banging?

A: Head banging is a way some babies use to get their parents to stop unwanted behavior (like teaching them to sleep through the night). It's extremely rare that a child will actually be hurt in the process, so resist the temptation to try to prevent it through intervention or adding pillows to a crib, for example. Aside from this deliberate head banging on the side of the crib, some babies softly bang their head rhythmically against the crib rails as a form of self-soothing. This sort of head banging usually starts after six months and can continue until a child is two years old. Most children outgrow it by the time they are three, and it can be a short-lived phase (a few months) or a longer time (several years). In rare cases, head banging can be a sign of a developmental or emotional problem, so if you notice it in other areas of your baby's life aside from the crib, it's a good idea to speak to your child's pediatrician.

Q: I'm pretty sure my child is afraid of the dark. What can I do? Will a night-light help?

A: Fear of the dark does not usually rear its head until two years of age, and for many children, it is never an issue. Before then, most children don't have the cognitive ability to be afraid of something so abstract. Usually when children put up a fight about the dark, it's most likely not fear, but words that they know will trigger you to respond. In our experience, children sleep better in a dark room, but if your child is older and your intuition is telling you that it's possible your child is afraid of the dark, you have two choices: add a night-light or give her a flashlight.

If you decide to add a light source, keep in mind that this can contribute to sleeping issues. Children who can see around their room are sometimes stimulated by the light and all their toys, so they will play instead of going to sleep. The other option is opening the door a crack and having a hallway light on. If you think your baby is starting to show signs of being afraid of the dark, you can remind her that she's safe and living in a wonderful home where her mommy and daddy love her so much, and that you're not concerned because there's nothing to be afraid of. Of course, be respectful; don't tell her that her fear is silly. When your baby sees that you are okay and not concerned, she'll feel better. A lot of times babies aren't sure what to think, so they look to us. Think about your son in a playground. He falls, and there's a thud. Everything's totally fine until you say in dismay, "Oh no!" Then he starts crying because he got the feedback he needed—that he should feel scared or hurt. If you believe that your child is safe, communicate that message rather than going to great lengths to protect your baby from the darkness.

Q: What's the difference between a nightmare and a night terror? What can I do about either?

A: Nightmares are frightening dreams and generally do not usually occur in children under eighteen months of age. They are often the result of stressful experiences, adjustment issues, or language development. Depending on their age and capacity for language, children can often recount elements of their nightmares. When it comes to handling nightmares, remain calm and neutrally supportive. You can limit any potentially scary experiences such as television, but you can't prevent nightmares from happening.

Night terrors are sleep disturbances where children seem to awaken screaming and in extreme fear, although they are not fully awake and often will not recall having a terror the next day. Terrors are thought to be caused by sleep deprivation, stressful life events, fever, or medications. They usually occur only in older children (three years or older) and are often the result of disrupted stage 3 (deep sleep) or 4 (more intense deep sleep). The distinguishing characteristic of night terrors is that children appear awake but do not respond to you. They also do not remember having a terror. Night terrors tend to happen when a child is overly tired or sick, or if one of his sleep cycles was interrupted. They may also happen for no apparent reason. It's best to calmly support him by sitting close by and gently stroking your child's back until the episode wanes rather than try to awaken him.

If your child is prone to night terrors, try to make sure he gets sufficient sleep and that his sleep schedule is consistent.

Feeding

Q: Won't my milk supply decrease if my baby goes eleven to twelve hours without a feeding at night?
A: Many breast-feeding moms don't realize that their milk supply decreases when they are exhausted and that getting more sleep can help boost supply. Once you start sleep teaching, you should not need to wake up in the middle of the night to pump. If your baby is sleeping at night, then you should too. However, it's a good idea to help communicate to your body that it should keep milk production up even when you are off the clock, so to speak. Assuming you nurse your child before you put her to sleep, it's helpful to pump twice before bed: once immediately after you put your baby to sleep and then one last time before you go to sleep for the night. In the morning, your breasts will feel very full—which is great, because your baby is hungry and primed for a big feed. If you are

still full after this feeding, pump again to completely empty each breast. Expect a few odd days as your body adjusts. But doing these extra pumpings will keep your supply up and recalibrate your production for daytime feedings.

Q: Is breast milk less filling than formula?

A: Breast milk and standard infant formula have the same caloric content (twenty calories per ounce). However, breast milk is easier for babies to digest, so it may not stick with them as long. Also, there are different types of breast milk: foremilk and hindmilk. Babies first reach the foremilk, then the hindmilk. Hindmilk is much fattier and therefore much more satisfying than foremilk, so if your baby is snacking on the breast all day long and not draining the entire breast, she will be hungry more often. If you are able to spread the breast milk feedings out to at least three hours apart during the day, then you should be confident that your exclusively breast-fed baby is getting both foremilk and hindmilk.

Q: What do you think about feeding a baby who is in a light state of sleep?

A: We aren't proponents of these so-called dream feeds (although we love the name) once parents begin sleep teaching. In case you're not familiar with dream feeds, they are generally given during the night, right before parents go to sleep themselves. The thought is that it will fill the baby up so she won't wake up an hour after you go to sleep. If your child is under four months and dream feeds are helping you get better sleep, that's great. Keep doing whatever is helping you at this time. However, we don't advocate dream feeds after four months of age because your child is now old enough to go through the night without eating. Also, eating at night kicks their digestive systems into third gear when it should be on cruise control. It causes poopy diapers and can exacerbate reflux issues.

Q: My baby is eight months old and only fifteen pounds. If I eliminate my nighttime feed I'm afraid she'll lose weight.

A: By four months, almost all full-term healthy babies can go eleven to twelve hours at night without a feeding. A good measure of health is your baby's ability to maintain her own growth curve—be that at the ninety-fifth, fiftieth, or tenth percentile. Also, at this age, a child should be eating three meals of solids as a complement to her daily milk feedings. Given all of this, it's incredibly unlikely that she truly needs to eat at night. She may be accustomed to eating, but it's not a requirement. It will actually serve her well to stop the feedings so both your body and her digestive system can get some rest at night. If you are still concerned, give yourself some peace of mind: check with your child's doctor and confirm that you can drop nighttime feedings. Our guess is that once she stops waking to eat, she will be better rested and will be able to eat more throughout the day. When you do drop nighttime feeds, expect some protesting. And honestly, who can blame her? If someone was willing to come to our bedside and give us a little bowl of mint chip ice cream during the night, we could probably get used to it pretty quickly. And although we don't need it, we'd probably put up a fight if it were taken away.

Sleep Teaching

Q: We live in an apartment complex where the walls are like paper. How can we sleep-teach?
A: First, try to start sleep teaching on a Friday because most people won't have work the next day. Then make the rounds on your floor. Tell your neighbors about your plan to sleep-teach. Give them the details about when you are starting, and explain that they may hear a few nights of protesting. You may want to sweeten the deal by bringing over a bottle of wine or some freshly baked cookies. Everyone will understand, especially when they see how exhausted you are.

Q: Is it better to make changes all at once or introduce them gradually? Would it be better to work on naps and night sleep separately, or is it better to do at the same time?
A: In our opinion, the less time our babies cry, the better. And when babies experience change, no matter how insignificant, they

usually cry. If we had the ability to communicate with our babies that one particular change is easier than another one, then gradual change would be less stressful for our children. Unfortunately, all babies see is change. It's black and white. So while it may make sense to us as adults to make gradual changes because we can see shades of gray, to a child it feels like they can never relax because they never know when the last change is going to come. Plus, you won't be able to fix sleep until you completely remove all the negative sleep associations, so your baby is not going to understand that you think she should be able to sleep independently. If you make the right changes once and don't change the goal once she reaches it, she'll gain self-esteem and a deeper trust in you.

Q: I want to teach my baby to sleep, but my partner is very against crying of any sort. What can I do?

A: We strongly recommend you and your partner talk out your differences before you attempt any sleep teaching. Sensitivity to crying is often about something else, and talking about our feelings is productive. If you attempt sleep teaching without the support of your partner, it'll not only be much more difficult for you, but your child will be affected because at some point your partner will be left in charge of your child and may respond differently than you would. An inconsistent response is incredibly frustrating to children because they never know what others want from them.

Q: Are there any special considerations for sleep-teaching adopted children?

A: Because many parents adopt children when they are newborns, there should be very little difference in how you approach sleep teaching if you wait until your baby is four months old. However, if you adopt a baby who is three months or older, we recommend that you wait a month or two before you attempt any sort of sleep teaching. When you bring your new baby home, focus on bonding and consistency so your baby can have time to learn that you are a constant, loving force in his life. Waiting a bit will also allow you the time to feel confident that you understand your baby's needs. In addition, you should never feel forced to separate at night before you are ready. But sometimes adopted babies are anxious and overly stimulated due to all the changes they have experienced in their short lives. Therefore, many have a hard time falling asleep. If this is the case, try to be as patient as possible. Getting some good rest will help your child start relaxing as well as catching up on any backed-up milestones. And getting into a consistent sleeping and feeding schedule will help your baby feel secure. Follow your instincts, and remember there is no need to rush into sleep teaching. People wait for various reasons all the time. And just because your baby is adopted doesn't mean that you are going to be judged by anyone for not fixing sleep right away. If you're preparing for the arrival of your new baby, you may not know how you are going to feel. So do what we recommend to all of our other expecting families and set up the room environment (see Chapter Three) to encourage safe and solid rest.

Q: When can I sleep-teach my preemie? She was born six weeks early.

A: If your baby was born more than two weeks premature but is otherwise healthy and thriving, you can still follow our sleep advice. However, you'll need to adjust your child's age so it is gestationally correct. Therefore, your child will need to be five and a half months (four months plus a six-week gestational correction) before we recommend starting any sort of sleep teaching. As always, before you start sleep teaching, check with your child's pediatrician to confirm that there is no reason that your baby shouldn't be able to sleep through the night.

Q: Can I sleep-teach if my baby has a gastrointestinal issue such as acid reflux or a milk intolerance?

A: Yes—if your baby is being treated by a physician. Sleep teaching will be an uphill battle if your child has a digestive condition that is not being managed. If you suspect your child has a GI or reflux issue, you should speak to her pediatrician. Signs your child may have acid reflux include crankiness when lying flat on her back,

arching during feedings, excessive spitting up, and possibly conges-
tion. Milk intolerance symptoms also include excessive spitting up
and fussiness, but also loose stools or blood or mucus in stools. If
your doctor is treating your baby, then trust that he or she has prescribed the suitable medication. Your baby may still be acting fussy,
but this may be because she isn't getting good sleep. If, after the first
week of sleep teaching, you continue to have multiple rousings or
long bouts of crying in the middle of the night, it may mean that
your baby's GI issue or reflux is not being adequately treated.

Q: I have several children of different ages, and it's impossible for my baby to sleep in a crib for all of her naps because I'm
constantly on the go. Can your advice still apply?

A: Yes! However, it may require you to do some extra work.
For the first two weeks of sleep teaching, find a way to put your baby
first. She has probably been very good about sharing your attention
and patiently sitting in her car seat during soccer practices. Being
part of a family is all about accommodating each other from time to
time. So during sleep teaching, your baby is your priority. Call in
favors from friends. Skip a class or two. Do whatever you need to
let your baby sleep in her crib during the learning. After she learns,
it's okay to stretch her sleep schedule (within reasonable limits). We
know you have to be flexible sometimes.

Q: How can I sleep-teach when my kids share a room?

A: We do not recommend having a child who isn't sleeping
through the night in the same room as another child. Instead, it's
best for your baby to share your sleeping space. When you do decide
to sleep-teach your baby, it is best to give your sleep learner his own
space in which to learn. Sometimes parents transform an office into
a temporary nursery or move out of their room into the living room
and keep the baby in their room for the first few nights. Whatever
you decide, make arrangements that you can live with for an extended
period of time. Every baby learns at a different pace. Once your baby
is sleeping well and you decide to move the children into the same
room, it's helpful to get something to separate them when sleep is

supposed to be happening. We like a curtain on a ceiling track. That way you don't have to worry about it falling over, and during the daytime it can be easily pulled back to open up the space.

Q: Is our two year old too old for sleep teaching?

A: It's never too late to teach your child how to sleep in a new way. That said, toddlers and preschoolers can be a bit more resistant to change and are more skilled in the area of parental manipulation. If you find your toddler really resisting sleep teaching, ensure that your daytime parenting matches your new nighttime parenting rules. What we mean is if at night, no means no and you are firm about her sleeping independently, make sure you follow the same protocol during the day. Some parents feel bad for being strict at night, so they compensate by caving during the day and letting their kids call all the shots. Inconsistent parents confuse children. As a result, many children hold on to the hope that they can call the shots at night too if they protest loudly or long enough.

Q: When is the best day to start sleep teaching?

A: Start sleep teaching only when you can commit to having your baby sleep in her crib (or a consistent place, like her crib at day care) for all naps and nighttime sleep for two weeks straight. This means not traveling anywhere during those two weeks. Generally we suggest starting on a Thursday or Friday night since the first few days of sleep teaching may be physically and emotionally trying. Many working families take the next day off so they can spend the day with their baby. That way, most spouses are home during the weekend and the parents can provide their children with ample support during waking hours.

Q: I'm doing sleep teaching, and my child is exhausted—the most tired I've seen him. Is this normal?

A: Yes, this is totally normal. We like to remind our parents of the end of the semester in college when you are cramming for finals and writing papers all night long. When you finally get home, you become a temporary couch potato, sleeping sixteen hours a day and barely moving. This is because your body is finally allowed to start catching up and you feel sleepy all the time. But once you get the rest you need and your parents have given you some healthy meals, you start to come out of your coma.

Your baby needs some space to recover, and you will too. Many of our parents know they should be happy that their baby is sleeping and should be more alert and fun during the day but they aren't. This is also totally normal. No one (even your baby) can make up for sleep deprivation in only a few days. It takes months sometimes. But each day you and your baby will start to feel better and better and much more energetic. And one day you are going to wake up and realize that that tired, boring person wasn't really you. You are the same fun person you used to be who could carry on conversations with others and didn't have to fake-laugh at jokes. When you see how easy it is to get a baby sleeping and then one day you wake up and realize you are the old you, you will have insight into the unnecessary toll that sleep deprivation has on families.

Q: How long will sleep teaching take to work? My son still cries at naptime.

A: Learning to sleep independently is a skill, and all children learn at different paces. Your child will be learning new skills every day during the initial two weeks of sleep teaching. Some children make a lot of quick improvement, but after a few days of consistency, they catch on to your attempt to take over and might resist longer than others. Whether you have a sensitive sleeper or a more willful child, your baby will get through all the important lessons if you keep believing in him and sticking to a consistent schedule. After two weeks, you can start to experiment with more flexibility. However, the fewer things you change, the easier his life will be for him in the long run. It can be disheartening for parents when children resist or struggle longer than others, but no baby is a lost cause when it comes to sleep. Healthy sleep (both daytime and nighttime) is the foundation for emotional and cognitive well-being. Any short-term frustration will be paid back in the grand scheme of your child's life. Keeping the big picture in mind is best for everyone.

Q: Why does a baby continue to cry for a bit of time at bedtime even though the sleep teaching appears to be mostly sticking?

A: A few things could be happening. First, you could have a particularly willful child who is having a hard time accepting change. Second, your response to your child could be inconsistent in some way, so there is a window of hope that things could go back to the way they once were (you, exhausted and rocking your baby to sleep throughout the day and night). Third, some children always cry a little bit before drifting off to sleep. Think of it as letting go of steam from the day before conking out. While it may be disturbing for you, if that's part of how he winds down, that's okay.

Q: What should we do if our baby throws her special sleep lovey out of her crib? Do we give it back?

A: This does happen from time to time. If your child tosses her sleep buddy aside and out of reach, it could have been an honest mistake. If you suspect this has happened (or can see in on a video monitor), wait five minutes and then return it without saying anything. This is what we call our one-time pass rule. However, if she throws it out a second time, limits are being tested and she is likely engaging in a game. It's hard to do, but it's best to not return it, leaving your child without it until the next sleep period. If it happens again, which is rare, you do the same thing: a one-time pass and then going without for the remaining sleep time. If you notice that this starts to happen each time you put your baby to bed, it is best to stop the game and omit the one time pass, leaving the lovey on the floor until the next sleeping period.

Crying

Q: Won't it make me seem like a bad parent if I just listen to my baby cry?

A: No one enjoys hearing a child cry, especially your own. We're certainly not immune to crying when it comes to our kids. But if you have set your child up for sleep teaching success with our prework, then you can be confident that your child is only frustrated by the change—especially if you have just started sleep teaching. Sometimes parents have to set limits and make unpopular choices when it is in their children's best interest. But once your child succeeds and discovers you were right, his trust in you and your respect for him multiply. We think you should feel good about that!

Q: Will crying hurt my child?

A: It's very rare for a baby to learn to sleep through the night without shedding some tears. Most mothers (including us) completely melt when their own children cry. That's because we are biologically programmed to respond this way. When you feel the urge to rescue your crying baby, run through your checklist. If nothing obvious is going on (sick, hurt, hungry, poopy diaper), it's helpful to remember that crying is a baby's only way of communicating for the first year or so of life. And remember too that babies don't always want or need your help when they cry. They could be dreaming, letting off some steam, or simply expressing frustration about something. If you run in and rescue your baby for being frustrated or letting off steam, you communicate that she always needs your help when she feels this way. However, if you give your baby a little space, she may find she can help herself sometimes. Studies have conclusively shown the positive effects of good sleep on mood, intelligence, and family well-being. As long as you give your child ample attention and love throughout the day, it will not harm your child to let her be frustrated at bedtime.

Q: My baby throws up if I let him cry. What do I do?

A: This is an understandably difficult situation, and we honestly don't like answering this question because there's no good answer. That said, some parents have this problem so we will address the ugly truth. Some children have an easy gag reflex, and for various reasons, they may be more disposed to throwing up. Some babies can also intentionally make themselves throw up if they know it gets them what they want (say, taken out of the crib).

Most children are far less likely to get sick if you finish all feedings, both solids and milk, at least one hour before bedtime. Many people feed their baby right before bed, thinking they're less likely to be hungry during the night. But if you put a baby who has a newly full stomach in the crib and he becomes frustrated for one reason or another, it's easy to see how he might throw up. Unfortunately, other than giving your child some time to digest his last meal before bed, there's not much more you can do to stop your child from throwing up if he gets upset.

The best way to handle this situation, however it occurs during sleep teaching, is to remain calm. Remember that the more excited you are, the more rewarded he is for the behavior and the more likely he is to do it again. If during a crib check you discover your child has thrown up, leave the room and grab your partner to help you with a cleanup. Try not to turn on the light in the room; instead use the light from the hallway. One of you cleans up the baby while the other changes the sheets. Then place your child back in bed like you did at bedtime. It's best not to talk to each other or your child if possible.

Napping

Q: My child is a great night sleeper but doesn't nap. What's going on?

A: If your child used to be a good napper but now is not, she may just be testing limits or asking for more control in her life. Sometimes, however, children are naturally very good at sleeping during the night because this is when their circadian rhythm is set to sleep for the longest period. If your baby has trouble napping, chances are that she has some negative sleep associations. Although these associations aren't preventing her from getting nighttime sleep, chances are they will crop up at night at some point. The best way to fix the nap is by looking at the full twenty-four-hour sleep picture. Start by removing any negative sleep associations at night sleep so that she has practice sleeping in this new way during a time when it is easier for her to sleep.

Q: What do I do if my child refuses to nap in her crib?

A: We hear this complaint from many parents. Many children who have problems sleeping during the day are especially sensitive to light or have a hard time winding down or making transitions. You can give your child a heads-up that a sleep time is approaching by doing an abbreviated version of your usual bedtime routine before the nap. This could be as simple as changing her diaper, putting her in more comfortable sleeping clothes, and singing the same song you sing before bed. Also, we advise parents facing nap challenges to make sure their child's room is as dark as possible by installing room-darkening curtains or using garbage bags taped to windows temporarily. This visual indication that it's sleep time can help children settle down quickly. Remember that daytime sleep is just as important and not all that different from nighttime sleep. If you fix nighttime sleep first and make naptime consistent with nighttime, your baby will learn. It might take up to two weeks for her to learn, but if you're consistent and give her a chance, she'll eventually catch on.

Q: How do you know when it's time to drop a nap?

A: You'll know that your baby is ready to drop this nap when she begins resisting it day after day for at least a week straight, without any extenuating circumstances (illness, life transition, milestone). This typically occurs after the one-year mark, but be careful not to jump the gun. A few days of nap resistance isn't a clear indication that it's time to change things.

Odds and Ends

Q: I understand why white noise is helpful, but can a baby become addicted to it?

A: The truth is that white noise will become a sleep association, but it's a positive one that will act as a sleep sign so your child can let go of any negative associations he might have. White noise is not harmful and usually makes bedtime a lot easier on a family. It cuts out much of the ambient noise around the house so your baby is not as prone to rousing and you don't need to tiptoe around and whisper. But as parents, we know that there will be times when you are traveling, forgot to pack white noise, and need your child to nap on the go. Be confident that your child can still sleep without the white noise; it might just be a little harder for him if he is used to it. If you're really worried about it, use it until your baby is sleeping well and then gradually decrease the volume over time. If your child starts rousing or has trouble traveling, you may want to increase the volume slightly, then start to decrease it again later.

Q: Teething wreaks havoc on my child's sleep. What can I do to avoid creating bad habits when she is in so much pain and I feel that I need to help her sleep?

A: We are asked about sleeping and teething issues from parents a lot, and for good reason. Cutting an entire mouthful of teeth is a long process—two to three years—and the experience of teething varies from child to child. Some babies are very sensitive teethers, while others pop out tooth after tooth without any evidence of suffering. Typically the most painful teething period lasts one to three days. During this time, use cool teething toys during the day and homeopathic teething tablets or a pain reliever (as prescribed by your pediatrician) at night. If you decide to use a pain reliever, give it about fifteen minutes before bedtime so it has time to take effect. If a very painful teething episode occurs during the first two weeks of sleep teaching, don't ignore it, but don't abandon teaching either. You can be more responsive than usual to make sure your baby is okay, but remember that your baby can still go back to sleep even though she is teething, especially with the help of pediatrician-approved pain relievers. This heightened pain should subside in a couple of days. If you have done your crib checks in as unexciting and quiet a manner as possible, you shouldn't have significant setbacks.

Q: My child is used to going to bed at 11:00 P.M. How can I make my child's bedtime earlier?

A: The best fix for little night owls is to use daytime naps to your advantage. If you can establish a consistent, age-appropriate nap schedule, you can prime your baby for the bedtime you want him to have. Remember that babies don't always know best. They often need you to guide them to what's best for them. Children between four and six months should be awake for the three hours leading up to bedtime. Those over six months should be awake for approximately four hours leading up to bedtime. Their bodies will adjust to a new schedule if you are consistent. If your baby is not accustomed to being awake for three to four hours in the evening, prepare yourself. It may be hard keeping him awake until bedtime for the first few days, but he will adjust.

Q: How can I get my child to sleep past 5:00 A.M.?

A: Early morning wakings can be very difficult for both children and parents. The good news is that most children who seem to be early risers really do want to go back to sleep. They just need someone to give them space to learn how to do it. When you're ready to teach your child to do this, follow all the steps in our sleep teaching chapters and start teaching at bedtime. That way, your child will have all the tools she needs at 5:00 A.M. when she rouses and needs to go back to sleep on her own. If you've already done sleep teaching, remember that lighter sleep takes place in the last few hours of nighttime sleep, so children awaken more easily. For that reason, it's a good idea to prevent outside distracters from sending a signal that the day has started. We suggest installing thick room-darkening shades and using white noise to help keep it looking and sounding like sleep time.

Q: Should I change a wet or poopy diaper in the night?

A: Most children can't fall asleep with a poopy diaper, and honestly, most parents don't want them to. The good news is that once children stop eating at night, they usually don't poop at night. However, they will have wet diapers. We do not encourage parents to change wet diapers. Today's diapers are very effective at locking away wetness, so your child will be comfortable. However, some children are prone to leaky diapers. If that's the case, you have to change their clothes (and sometimes sheet) because they can get cold if they are wet. To prevent further leaky diapers, try superabsorbent overnight diapers first. If that still doesn't work, you can try our double diaper recipe, which we provide in Chapter Eleven.

Q: What's your stance on pacifiers?

A: Pacifiers can be very helpful when children are very young. Many have a strong need to suck, and pacifier sucking is thought to help prevent sudden infant death syndrome. However, once it's time to sleep-teach, the choice to use a pacifier is a complicated one. The truth is that most parents are incredibly concerned about getting rid of the pacifier. However, we've never met a family that wasn't shocked at how quickly their baby adapted to life without one. The bottom line is that if your child can't put a pacifier in her mouth on her own in the dark, you shouldn't give her a pacifier while sleep teaching. If you do, she'll need your help at night to reinsert it. If you absolutely cannot imagine getting rid of the pacifier, it's possible to sleep-teach with a pacifier. But if this is the case, you should wait to begin sleep teaching until your baby can put a pacifier in her mouth without your help, typically at six months or older. The only problem with this situation is that a pacifier is pretty small and can be hard to find in the dark. That means your baby is going to have to rouse more and become more fully awake between sleep cycles, which makes it harder for her to put herself back to sleep. For whatever value you hope to add by keeping the pacifier, there is an equally unsavory consequence. For these reasons, we strongly recommend that you not use the pacifier once you begin sleep teaching.

Q: My child snores. Is this normal?

A: It depends. Snoring can be normal and is often associated with temporary illnesses like colds. In cases where snoring is persistent, severe, or associated with irregular gasps, it may be a sign of allergies or an even more serious condition like sleep apnea. Adding an air purifier may help snoring due to allergies. But if you suspect sleep apnea, consult with your pediatrician immediately.

Q: My baby used to sleep through the night but has begun waking several times. When I go into his room, all I have to do is rub his back and he falls back to sleep. What's going on?

A: It sounds as if your baby may be experiencing the beginning of separation anxiety. Some parents are frustrated when this stage happens, but it's normal and a healthy part of your child's development. It means your baby has the cognitive ability to understand that you exist even when he can't see you. Your baby will eventually become more comfortable with his newfound awareness. In the meantime, stop the back rubbing at night (which is a negative sleep association) and instead help your child by giving him opportunities to practice separating from you during the day (even for a minute) and find a way to separate from your child each week even if it's only for an hour or so. Pick a consistent time each week, and make sure your child sees you getting ready to leave your home. He may protest at first, but resist the temptation to sneak out. In fact, involve him in the process of leaving. As you put on your coat, be upbeat and say something like, "Mommy is leaving, but she'll be back soon!"

Q: I have twins. One sleeps through the night, while the other wakes up to eat. How do I get them in sync?

A: Just because your children shared a womb for the better part of a year does not mean they will be instantly compatible roommates once they arrive. Twins can be as different as night and day. That said, many parents want twins to be on the same schedule and share a room. We recommend that you do put them on the same eating and sleeping schedule because it will make your life much more manageable. In terms of sharing a room, it's easiest for you to teach them how to be independent sleepers in separate rooms. So for sleep teaching, separate them for a week or so. Once they're both sleeping, move them back in the room together but in separate cribs.

Q: Our daughter fights sleep all day, sometimes falls asleep during her bedtime, and sometimes stays up for another hour. What's going on? Why is her sleep so irregular?

A: This is the description of a typical baby who isn't getting the benefit of a good night's sleep. The first thing we recommend is to choose a consistent bedtime, wake-up time, and naptime. Check out the schedules that we recommend by gestational age in Chapter Five. If you can get your baby on a consistent, age-appropriate schedule it will be easier for you to know when she should be napping during the day. Right now you may be missing signs of your child's sleepiness throughout the day. When your child misses her sleep window and becomes overly tired, she can become more difficult to put to bed. Once you give her consistency and some positive sleep associations, she'll start to love sleep just the way the rest of us do.

Sleep Teaching Overview

We created this summary of our sleep approach primarily for other caregivers. However, it's a good reminder for parents too. If everyone is consistent, your child will have an easier time learning to love sleep. We recommend posting this in a prominent place. If your child goes to day care, we encourage you to share this overview with your child-care providers. They may not be able to follow it exactly given their setup, but many parents are pleasantly surprised at how accommodating some providers can be.

1. *Consistent schedule.* See the posted schedule, and keep the child on track.

2. *Milk feedings.* Give at the scheduled feeding times, but not in his or her in sleeping space.

3. *Nap guidelines.* Follow these instructions:

    ✓ No stroller or car seat naps during sleep teaching.
    ✓ Mini-routine before naps (for example, comfortable clothes on, one book, one song). Put baby in the crib awake.
    ✓ If baby falls asleep before naptime, wake up and proceed with naptime as usual later.
    ✓ If baby cries going down for nap, listen for highs and lows. Do crib checks only as necessary.

If baby wakes up early from nap, give him a chance to fall asleep until his designated wake-up time. Limit crying to one hour in duration.

4. *Sleeping space.* Same environment for both naps and bedtime. Use this checklist:

- ✓ Child in comfortable sleeping attire
- ✓ Correct temperature (sixty-eight to seventy-two degrees)
- ✓ Room-darkening curtains or shades closed or pulled
- ✓ White noise turned on
- ✓ Lovey in crib (no other toys)
- ✓ Door closed

5. *Crib checks.* Crib checks are a brief check on a child to make sure she is safe. Hands down, if you hear a cry that makes you worry your child's safety or health is at risk, go in and do a crib check. Or if you start to feel a strong desire to make sure your baby is okay, try to wait five minutes before doing a crib check. If the baby is still crying and you are still concerned, then do a crib check. Your visit is very brief (thirty seconds) and boring. Enter the child's room, do not turn on lights, do not talk, pat, or even make eye contact. Look over the child and smell for a poopy diaper. Make sure the white noise machine is still on. Fix anything amiss quickly, but if everything is okay, then you can be confident that the baby is working on putting himself to sleep and you can leave the room.

6. *Wake-up party.* Give an enthusiastic wake-up party at the end of each nap or beginning of each day. Enter the nursery happy and excited, saying something like, "Yay! Great job, Lily! Time to wake up and play! Woo-hoo!" Do this every time her nap or nighttime sleep is over, even if she struggled to nap or didn't nap at all.

7. *Awake times.* Fill awake times with lots of love, attention, and fun. Get outside, and if possible, interact with other children.

Worksheet Templates

Worksheet 1: Sleeping and Eating Log

Creating a record of your child's tendencies before sleep teaching will be instrumental in creating a sleep plan. We have provided an example of a filled-in log for your reference here. We recommend you use the blank log provided on the next page and record your child's eating and sleeping patterns for three consecutive days before you begin sleep teaching. This will give you a sense of his normal food intake and clues about his sleep associations. The log is also available for downloading; see the Book tab on our Web site at www.dreamteambaby.com.

Sleeping and Eating Log

Date: August 5

Time	Activity (i.e., sleeping, eating, fussing)	Notes
7:30 am	Woke up and nursed	
9:00 am	2 oz. cereal + 1 oz. prunes	
10:00 am	Acting tired, refused breast	
11:00–11:45 am	Nap in stroller	Woke up when ambulance drove by
2:30 pm	Bottle (breast milk, 4 oz.)	
3:45–5:00 pm	Nap in crib	
5:30 pm	Bottle (breast milk, 4 oz.)	Still seemed hungry, but refused additional bottle
6:45–7:15 pm	Nap in stroller	
7:15 pm	2 oz. sweet potatoes + 1 oz. green beans	
8:45 pm	Bath	
9:15 pm	Bottle (formula, 5 oz.)	
12:30 am	Woke-up	Cried, replaced paci, fell asleep in 10 minutes
2:30 am	Woke-up	Nursed 4 minutes
4:30 am	Woke-up	Let cry 5 minutes, then nursed 2 minutes

Appendix C

Sleeping and Eating Log

Date:

Time	Activity (i.e., sleeping, eating, fussing)	Notes

Worksheet 2: Contract for Sleep Teaching

Before you embark on sleep teaching, it's important to sit down with your partner for a heart-to-heart talk. Fill out this contract together and list five to ten "nurture items"—things that make each partner feel nurtured. This way, you'll have a clear understanding of how to support each other during the tough times.

Earlier in this book, we stressed the importance of lining up an emotional support system to help you throughout the sleep teaching process. Consider this worksheet as your second-tier support. If you or your partner find at any point that you want to give up, look back on this contract to restore your confidence, remind you of your obligation to nurture your partner, and give you the focus you need to keep going.

Parent 1: _____

Reasons for sleep teaching
  1.
  2.
  3.
  4.
  5.

Things that make me feel nurtured
  1.
  2.
  3.
  4.
  5.
  6.
  7.
  8.
  9.
  10.

I, _____, dedicate the next two weeks to teaching my child to sleep. It may be frustrating, and I may want to give up. I will keep the big picture in mind and remember that sleep is a gift I'm giving to my child.

Signature: _____

Parent 2:_____

Reasons for sleep teaching

1.
2.
3.
4.
5.

Things that make me feel nurtured

1.
2.
3.
4.
5.
6.
7.
8.
9.
10.

I, _____, dedicate the next two weeks to teaching my child to sleep. It may be frustrating, and I may want to give up. I will keep the big picture in mind and remember that sleep is a gift I'm giving to my child.

Signature: _____

Worksheet 3: Your Child's Sleep Schedule

On this page is a sample filled-in sleep schedule. Customizable sleep schedules are available on our Web site. Visit www.dreamteambaby. com, click on the Book tab, and download yours for free. On the next page is blank sleep schedule for you to use.

Schedule for: _Cooper_

Age: _5 months_

Time	Activity
7:00 am	Wake up for the day!
7:15 am	Milk feed
8:00 am	Playtime inside
9:00 am	Nap #1
10:00 am	Wake from nap
10:15 am	Milk feed
10:45 am	Playtime outside!
12:00 pm	Nap #2
1:00 pm	Wake from nap
1:15 pm	Milk feed
1:40 pm	Playtime
3:00 pm	Nap #3
4:00 pm	Wake from nap
4:15 pm	Milk feed
6:00 pm	Bathed and dressed for bed
6:30 pm	Milk feed outside nursery
6:40 pm	Bedtime routine
7:00 pm	Bedtime

Classes and Activities

_____

_____

_____

_____

Schedule for:_____

Age:_____

Time	Activity

Classes and Activities

_____

_____

_____

_____

_____

Bootzin RR, Gomez RL, Hupbach A, Nadel L. Nap-dependent learning in infants. *Developmental Science*, 2009;12:1007–1012.

Chee MWL, Chuah LYM, Huettel S, Payne JW, Venkatraman V. Sleep deprivation biases the neural mechanisms underlying economic preferences. *Journal of Neuroscience*, 2011;31(10):3712–3718.

Schwichtenberg AJ, Anders TF, Vollbrecht M, Poehlmann J. Daytime sleep and parenting interactions in infants born preterm. *Journal of Developmental and Behavioral Pediatrics*, 2011;32(1):8–17.

Spruyt K, Aitken RJ, So K, Charlton M, Adamson TM, Horne RS. Relationship between sleep/wake patterns, temperament and overall development in term infants over the first year of life. *Early Human Development*, 2008;84(5):289–296.

Photo courtesy Ron Holtz.

Conner Herman and **Kira Ryan** are moms and lovers of sleep who, after unsuccessfully following the advice of countless sleep books, were convinced there was a better way to teach babies how to sleep through the night. They recruited a board of experts to tap their collective knowledge on sleep and created Dream Team Baby, a unique approach to sleep teaching. Today their Dream Team helps thousands of babies and their parents across the country get some well-deserved sleep.

Conner and Kira are also the sleep experts for The Bump.com, a national parenting resource, and have appeared on several national television programs, including *The Today Show, The Early Show,* and *Good Morning America,* along with some programs on ParentsTV. Their advice is regularly featured in parents' magazines, blogs, and other publications.

INDEX

Page references followed by *fig* indicate an illustrated figure; followed by *t* indicate a table.